9.03

D0614479

8

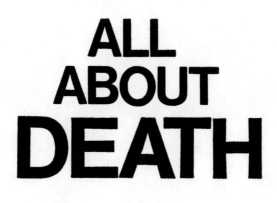

ALL
ABOUT
DEATH

Compiled by Peter Potter

A
BULL'S-EYE
BOOK

Published by
William Mulvey Inc.
72 Park Street
New Canaan, Conn. 06840

Cover design: Ted Palmer

Library of Congress Cataloging-in-Publication Data

All About Death
"A Bull's-eye Book"

1. Death—Quotations, maxims, etc.
I. Potter, Peter (date).

PN6084.D4A44   1988   082   86—43159

ISBN 0—934791—08—2

All Scriptural quotations are from the
King James Version of the Bible.
ABS 1967 KJ053—C Series—D—2

Printed in the United States of America
First Edition

Dedicated to the Clergy.
Men and Women who give their lives
so we can better know Jesus Christ.

Introduction

What lies ahead? After this life is there another one? If so, what will it be like?

For centuries great thinkers have considered these questions. And why not? Is there any more fundamental question, any greater mystery?

Here are hundreds of thoughts and observations on Death. I hope you find them interesting and stimulating.

Peter Potter

A

ACCEPTANCE
ASHES TO ASHES
A TIME FOR DYING

Acceptance

The name of death is terrible, as it is usually proposed to us, for someone says: "Your dear father is dead," or "Your son is dead." This is not well-spoken among Christians. We should say, "Your son or your father is gone to his country and to yours; and because necessity required it, he passed by the way of death, in which he lingered not."

Saint Francis of Sales

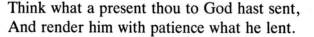

I define death as an arrest of life, from which no revival of any length, whether of the whole or of any part, can take place.

August Weisman

Never say about anything, "I have lost it," but only "I have given it back." Is your child dead? It has been given back. Is your wife dead? She has been returned.

Epictetus

Think what a present thou to God hast sent,
And render him with patience what he lent.

John Milton

In this life to die is nothing new; but then, there is nothing newer about living!

Sergei Esenin

It is man only who is able to face his death consciously; that belongs to his greatness and dignity. . . . Man's knowledge that he has to die is also man's knowledge that he is above death.

Paul Tillich

It is God's way. His will, not ours, be done.

William McKinley

No man can be ignorant that he must die, nor be sure that he may not this very day.

Cicero

If somebody wants to shoot me from a window with a rifle, nobody can stop it, so why worry about it.

John F. Kennedy

Death is a metaphor; nobody dies to himself.

Lawrence Durell

Death, the most dreaded of evils, is therefore of no concern to us, for while we exist death is not present, and when death is present we no longer exist.

Epicurus

We have made a covenant with death.

The Bible

Once you accept your own death all of a sudden you are free to live. You no longer care about your reputation . . . you no longer care except so far as your life can be used tactically—to promote a cause you believe in.

Saul Alinsky

The closer we come to the negative, to death, the more we blossom.

Montgomery Clift

I acquiesce in my death with complete willingness, uncoloured by hesitation; how foolish to cling to life when God has ordained otherwise.

Jorge Manrique

To die would be an awfully big adventure.

James M. Barrie

Ashes to Ashes

In the sweat of thy face shalt thou eat bread, till thou return unto the ground; for out of it wast thou taken: for dust thou art, and unto dust shalt thou return.

The Bible

Cities fall, kingdoms perish, their pride and pomp lie buried in sand and grass. Then why should mortal man repine to die, whose life is as air, breath as wind, and body as glass?

Torquato Tasso

———

All flesh shall perish together, and man shall turn again unto dust.

The Bible

———

A man, when he burns, leaves only a handful of ashes. No woman can hold him. The wind must blow him away.

Tennessee Williams

———

When our mortal frame shall be disjoin'd
The lifeless lump uncoupled from the mind,
From sense of grief and pain we shall be free,
We shall not feel, because we shall not be.

John Dryden

———

Man goeth to his long home, and the mourners go about the streets: or ever the silver cord be loosed, or the golden bowl be broken, or the pitcher be broken at the fountain, or the wheel broken at the cistern. Then shall the dust return to the earth as it was: and the spirit shall return unto God who gave it.

The Bible

Man has given a false importance to death. Any animal, plant, or man who dies adds to Nature's compost heap, becomes the manure without which, nothing could grow nothing could be created. Death is simply part of the process.

Peter Weiss

All things fall back into the earth and also arise from the earth.

Cicero

Where is the dust that has not been alive?
The spade, the plough, disturb our ancestors;
From human mould we reap our daily bread.

Edward Young

This quiet Dust was Gentlemen and Ladies,
    And Lads and Girls;
Was laughter and ability and sighing,
    And frocks and curls.

Emily Dickinson

A little season of love and laughter,
    Of light and life, and pleasure, and pain,
And a horror of outer darkness after.
    And the dust returneth to dust again.

Adam L. Gordon

The sun will rise, the winds that ever move
Will blow our dust that once were men in love.

John Masefield

We perish, we disappear, but the march of time goes on forever.

Ernest Renan

Earth to earth, ashes to ashes, dust to dust; in sure and certain hope of the Resurrection.

The Book of Common Prayer

A dead man is only a dead man and is of no importance.

Molière

A Time For Dying

Leaves have their time to fall,
And flowers to wither at the North wind's breath
And stars to set—but all,
Thou hast all seasons for thine own, O death.

Felicia Hemans

There is no man who does not die his own death . . . . No one dies except upon his own day.

Seneca

Death is a black camel that kneels once at every man's door.

Turkish proverb

We are but tenants, and . . . shortly the great Landlord will give us notice that our lease has expired.

Joseph Jefferson,
Instruction on his monument at Sandwich,
Cape Cod, Mass.

Death keeps no calendar.

George Herbert

Each has his appointed day; life is brief and irrevocable.

Virgil

The rising morn cannot assure
    That we shall end the day
For the Death stands ready at the door
    To take our lives away.

Anonymous

All has its date below; the fatal hour
Was register'd in Heav'n ere time began.
We turn to dust, and all our mightiest works
Die too.

William Cowper

No one can postpone the allotted day.

Seneca

All human things are subject to decay,
And when fate summons, monarchs must obey.

John Dryden

The best men cannot suspend their fate;
The good die early, and the bad die late.

Daniel Defoe

The Lord may not come when you want him, but he's always
going to be there on time.

Lou Gossett, Jr.

What is there astounding in the death of a mortal? But we are
grieved at his dying before his time. Are we sure that this was
not his time? We do not know how to pick and choose what is
good for our souls, or how to fix the limits of the life of man.

Saint Basil

When life knocks at the door no one can wait,
When Death makes his arrest we have to go.

John Masefield

One always dies too soon—or too late. And yet one's whole life is complete at that moment, with a line drawn neatly under it, ready for the summing up.

Jean-Paul Sartre

Man's happiest lot is to know when to die.

Lucan

There is a fullness of time when men should go, and not occupy too long the ground to which others have a right to advance.

Thomas Jefferson

One should die proudly when it is no longer possible to live proudly.

Friedrich Nietzsche

To die is to leave off dying and do the thing once for all.

Samuel Butler

B

BEFORE I WAKE

BELIEF

BE NOT PROUD

Before I Wake

Each night is but the past day's funeral, and the morning his resurrection: why then should our funeral sleep be otherwise than our sleep at night?

Arthur Warwick

Death, so called is a thing which makes men weep,
And yet a third of Life is passed in sleeping.

Lord Byron

Yet as with morn my lad finds fears were vain,
So death shall give to age its toys again.

John R. Moreland

Death is the veil which those who live call life:
They sleep, and it is lifted.

Percy Bysshe Shelley

What is death at most? It is a journey for a season; a sleep longer than usual. If thou fearest death, thou shouldest also fear sleep.

Saint John Chrysostom

We sometimes congratulate ourselves at the moment of waking from a troubled dream: it may be so at the moment of death.

Nathaniel Hawthorne

It is not without reason that we are taught to study even our sleep for the resemblance it has with death. How easily we pass from waking to sleeping! With how little sense of loss we lose consciousness of the light and of ourselves! Perhaps the faculty of sleep, which deprives us of all action and all feeling, might seem useless and contrary to nature, were it not that thereby Nature teaches us that she has made us for dying and living alike, and from the start of life presents to us the eternal state that she reserves for us after we die, to accustom us to it and take away our fear of it.

Michel de Montaigne

———

Her suffering ended with the day;
   Yet lived she at its close,
And breathed the long, long night away
   In statue-like repose.

But when the sun, in all his state,
   Illuminated the eastern skies,
She passed through Glory's morning gate,
   And walked in Paradise.

James Aldrich

———

How sweet—heavenly sweet—it is to be lulled into the sleep of death by one's beloved.

Johann C.F. von Schiller

Life! we've been long together
Through pleasant and through cloudy weather;
'Tis hard to part when friends are dear—
Perhaps 'twill cost a sigh, a tear;
Then steal away, give little warning,
  Choose thine own time;
Say not good night,—but in some brighter clime
Bid me good-morning.

Anna L. Barbauld

A little sleep, a little slumber, a little folding of the hands to sleep.

The Bible

I must sleep now.

Lord Byron, dying

So softly death succeeded life in her,
She did but dream of Heaven, and she was there.

John Dryden

Teach me to live that I may dread
The grave as little as my bed.

Thomas Ken

Father in thy gracious keeping
Leave me now thy servant sleeping.

John L. Ellerton

Belief

Every man knows he will die, but no man wants to believe it.

Hebrew proverb

God gave us the blessed hope of immortality, through which we may console ourselves for the vanity of life, and overcome the fear of death.

Jedaia Ben Bedersi

The hope of immortality is the most subjective of experiences. No one can prove it for us and no philosophical argument can convince us. It is, of course, a matter of faith which Easter bestows on those who have accepted Jesus Christ as Lord.

Gerald Kennedy

Socrates proved the immortality of the soul from the fact that sickness of the soul (sin) does not consume it as bodily sickness consumes the body.

Sören Kierkegaard

Almost every person I have ever talked to in my world travels has believed in life after death.

Eleanor Roosevelt

It is the sense of boundless possibilities in man which justifies faith in personal immortality.

William A. Brown

If I err in my belief that the soul of men are immortal, I err, gladly, and I do not wish to lose so delightful an error.

Cicero

I am a better believer, and all serious souls are better believers, in immortality than we can give grounds for.

Ralph Waldo Emerson

If I did not believe in a future state,
I should believe in no God.

John Adams

I have been greatly struck by the comparative silence which seems to have fallen on the belief in immortality, as an essential element of the Christian religion. . . . The general practice seems to be, not indeed to disavow the belief, but to keep it in cold storage for funeral occasions.

Lawrence P. Jacks

The belief of immortality is impressed upon all men, and all men act under an impression of it, however they may talk, and though, perhaps, they may be scarcely sensible of it.

Samuel Johnson

Neither experience nor science has given man the idea of immortality . . . . The idea of immortality rises from the very depths of his soul—he feels, he sees, he knows that he is immortal.

François Guizot

The notion of the survival of the spirit after death in some form, whether clear or vague, has ever existed in the human mind from the most primitive times to the present hour.

Henry Frank

Neither a man nor a nation can live without a "higher idea," and there is only one such idea on earth, that of an immortal human soul; all the other "higher ideas" by which men live follow from that.

Feodor Dostoevsky

The deeper our conviction of the rationality of the Universe, the stronger becomes our unwillingness to believe that such an order can be final and permanent. Hence it is that a sincere Theism has nearly always carried with it a belief in Immortality.

Hastings Rashdall

The doctrine of the immortality of the Soul is an integral part of the Jewish creed. It is more; it is a necessary ingredient of every consistent religious creed.

Morris Joseph

I believe in the immortality of the soul, not in the sense in which I accept the demonstrable truths of science, but as a supreme act of faith in the reasonableness of God's work.

John Fiske

Everything science has taught me—and continues to teach me—strengthens my belief in the continuity of our spiritual existence after death.

Werner von Braun

Believing in a God of infinite love and of infinite power, I find it natural to believe that death is not a disastrous sundown but rather a spiritual sunrise, ushering in the unconjectured splendors of immortality.

Archibald Rutledge

The immortality in which I declare my faith is uncompromisingly religious in concept. . . . I mean a personal immortality of this soul, this consciousness after a physical death on earth.

Hyman J. Schachtel

The blazing evidence of immortality is our dissatisfaction with any other solution.

Ralph Waldo Emerson

Be Not Proud

Death, be not proud, though some have called thee
Mighty and dreadful, for thou art not so,
For those whom thou think'st thou doest overthrow
Die not, poor Death, not yet canst thou kill me. . .
One short sleep past, we wake eternally,
And death shall be no more; Death, thou shalt die.

John Donne

Man is immortal and the body cannot die, because matter has no life to surrender. The human concept named matter, death, disease, sickness and sin are all that can be destroyed. Death is but another phase of the dream that existence can be material.

Mary Baker Eddy

Now among all passions inflicted from without, death holds the first place, just as sexual concupiscences are chief among internal passions. Consequently, when a man conquers death and things directed to death, his is a most perfect victory.

Saint Thomas Aquinas

The truest end of life is to know that life never ends. . . .
Death is no more than a turning of us over from time to eternity.

William Penn

The question whether our conscious personality survives after death has been answered by almost all races of men in the affirmative. On this point skeptical or agnostic people are nearly, if not wholly unknown.

James G. Frazer

Death cannot kill what never dies.

Thomas Traherne

Man, tree, and flower are supposed to die; but the fact remains that God's universe is spiritual and immortal.

Mary Baker Eddy

CERTAINTIES

Certainties

Death and taxes and childbirth! There's never any convenient time for any of them!

Margaret Mitchell

Death and vulgarity are the only two facts in the Nineteenth Century that one cannot explain away.

Oscar Wilde

Death and labour are things of necessity and not of choice.

Simone Weil

Of all impositions on the public the greatest seems to be death.

Leigh Hunt

Death visits each and all; the slayer soon follows the slain.

Seneca

We shall never outwit nature; we shall all die as usual.

Bernard Fontenelle

To die and to lose one's life are much the same thing.

Irish proverb

Everything on earth fades fast
Death will take us all at last.
That's a truth we know won't pass.

Georg Büchner

Mortality is not simply an avoidable accident, but a natural appointment, from which there is no hope of escape.

Jonathan Miller

Death is a law, not a punishment.

Jean-Baptiste Dubos

I'm not afraid of death. It's that stake one puts up in order to play the game of life.

Jean Giraudoux

Why, what is pomp, rule, reign, but earth and dust?
And, live we how we can, yet die we must.

Shakespeare

What does it matter when it comes, since it is inevitable?

Michel de Montaigne

A man dies still if he has done nothing, as one who has done much.

Homer

And every life, no matter if its hour is rich with love and every moment jeweled with joy, will, at its close, become a tragedy as sad and deep and dark as can be woven of the warp and woof of mystery and death.

Robert G. Ingersoll

Things have a terrible permanence when people die.

Joyce Kilmer

It is death that is the guide of our life, and our life has no goal but death.

Archibald MacLeish

For certain is death for the born, and certain is birth for the dead; therefore over the inevitable thou shouldst not grieve.

Bhagavad-Gita

In the long run we are all dead.

John Maynard Keynes

There is a remedy for everything but death, which will be sure to lay us out flat some time or other.

Cervantes

For ages, billions of fools, without number, in languages without number, have said again and again, with a knowing look, "When you're dead, you're dead."

George Bernanos

D

DAMNATION

DEATH'S STING

DEATH WATCHES

DEATH WISHES

DENIAL

DESPAIR

Damnation

And I looked, and behold a pale horse: and his name that sat on him was Death, and Hell followed with him. And power was given unto them over the fourth part of the earth, to kill with sword, and with hunger, and with death, and with the beasts of the earth.

The Bible

Man lieth down, and riseth not: till the heavens be no more, they shall not awake, nor be raised out of their sleep.

The Bible

The sorrows of hell compassed me.

The Bible

Death spoke and said: ". . .There is no future for the fool who seeks pleasure, who is befooled by love of wealth. This is the world, there is no other. If one thinks thus he comes again and again into my power."

Katha Upanishad

God has no need of marionettes. He pays men the compliment of allowing them to live without him in this life, they must also live without him in the next.

Leon Morris

All who go down to hell shall come up again, except these three: he who commits adultery, he who shames another in public, and he who gives another a bad name.

Baba Metzia

I know that at the end of this life some will do penance by purgatorial flames.

Saint Gregory I

Hell has three doors: lust, rage and greed.

Bhagavad-Gita

As the soul has passed beyond the time of merit it must suffer in Purgatory till the dross of sin is removed. It can do nothing but suffer.

Gerald C. Treacy

The fire of Gehenna is sixty times as hot as the fire of this earth.

The Talmud

A man will not be able to participate in divinity until the cleansing fire will have purged him of every fault which has found its way into his soul.

Saint Gregory of Nyssa

When thou art scorching in thy flames,
When thou art howling in thy torments,
Then God shall laugh, and His saints
Shall sing and rejoice, that His power
And Wrath are thus made known to thee.

Christopher Love

The dead praise not the Lord.

The Bible

We put ourselves there. The door to Hell is locked from the inside.

James A. Pike

Death is not the greatest loss in life. The greatest loss is what dies inside us while we live.

Norman Cousins

Death's Sting

All the doctrines that have flourished in the world about immortality have hardly affected men's natural sentiment in the face of death.

George Santayana

Life, like a dome of many-coloured glass,
   Stains the white radiance of Eternity.
Until Death tramples it to fragments.

                              Percy Bysshe Shelley

. . . Only the dead are free, the chain is broken . . . but perhaps they miss their chains?

                              Eeva-Liisa Manner

Death is the receipt for all evils.

                              Michel de Montaigne

We must needs die, and are as water spilt on the ground,
which cannot be gathered up again.

                              The Bible

To have to die is a distinction of which no man is proud.

                              Alexander Smith

Those who are nearly dead regret their approaching death
the most.

                              Jean de la Fontaine

O death, where is thy sting? O grave, where is thy victory?

                              The Bible

A protracted illness seems to prepare one for the end, though when it comes, even after months of illness, it always seems sudden and terrible. I think death is always terrible, even in what is looked upon as its most peaceful and calmest forms.

Basil W. Maturin

It is dreadful to feel all one possesses slipping away.

Blaise Pascal

So much to do; so little done!

Cecil Rhodes, dying

The deep pain that is felt at the death of every friendly soul arises from the feeling that there is in every individual something which is inexpressible, peculiar to him alone, and is, therefore, absolutely and irretrievably lost.

Arthur Schopenhauer

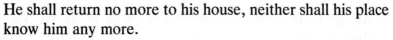

He shall return no more to his house, neither shall his place know him any more.

The Bible

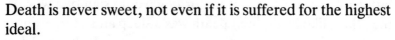

Death is never sweet, not even if it is suffered for the highest ideal.

Erich Fromm

Let children walk with Nature, let them see the beautiful blendings and communions of death and life, their joyous inseparable unity, as taught in woods and meadows, . . . and they will learn that death is stingless indeed, and as beautiful as life.

John Muir

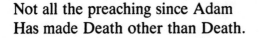

Not all the preaching since Adam
Has made Death other than Death.

James Russell Lowell

Death surprises us in the midst of our hopes.

Thomas B. Fuller

Death is always new.

West African proverb

Death Watches

I have careful records of about 500 deathbeds, studied particularly with reference to the modes of death and the sensations of the dying. . . . Ninety suffered bodily pain or distress of one sort or another, eleven showed mental apprehension, two positive terror, one expressed spiritual exaltation, one bitter remorse. The great majority gave no sign one way or the other; like birth, their death was a sleep and a forgetting.

William Osler

The dull nights go over, and the dull days also,
The soreness of lying so much in bed goes over,
The physician, after long putting off, gives the silent and terrible look for an answer.
The children come hurried and weeping, and the brothers and sisters are sent for.

Walt Whitman

We all look up to the blue sky for comfort, but nothing appears there, nothing comforts, nothing answers us, and so we die.

Samuel T. Coleridge

A man's dying is more the survivors' affair than his own.

Thomas Mann

It is not true that the dying man is generally more honest than the living. On the contrary, by the solemn attitude of the bystanders and the flowing or repressed streams of tears, everyone present is inveigled into a comedy of vanity, now conscious, now unconscious.

Friedrich Nietzsche

He pulls with a long rope that waits for another's death.

George Herbert

The dying are nearly as reticent as the dead.

Alexander

There is none so fortunate that there will not be one or two standing at his deathbed who will welcome the evil befalling him.

Marcus Aurelius

We are fools to depend upon the society of our fellowmen. Wretched as we are, powerless as we are, they will not aid us; we shall die alone.

Blaise Pascal

My name is death: the last best friend am I.

Robert Southey

If even dying is to be made a social function, then, please, grant me the favor of sneaking out on tiptoe without disturbing the party.

Dag Hammarskjold

Spare me the whispering, crowded room,
The friends who come and gape and go,
The ceremonious air of gloom—
All, which makes death a hideous show.

Matthew Arnold

Death is very sophisticated. It's like a Noel Coward comedy. You light a cigarette and wait for it in the library.

Theadora van Runkle

Take away but the pomps of death, the disguises, and solemn bugbears, and the actings by candlelight, and proper and phantastic ceremonies, the minstrels and the noisemakers, the women and the weepers, the swoonings and the shriekings, the nurses and the physicians, the dark room and the ministers, the kindred and the watchers, and then to die is easy, ready, and quitted from its troublesome circumstances.

Jeremy Taylor

Death Wishes

Death is what men want when the anguish of living is more than they can bear.

Euripides

There is no refuge from confession except in suicide and suicide is confession.

James Baldwin

Every suicide is a solution to a problem.

Jean Baechler

To attempt suicide is a criminal offense. Any man who, of his own will, tries to escape the treadmill to which the rest of us feel chained incites our envy, and therefore our fury. We do not suffer him to go unpunished.

Alexander Chase

He would have hastened his end but suicide would not have been a victory. Death was coming to him legitimately, as a justification, as a gift from life. That was his greatest triumph.

Flannery O'Connor

Death is a remedy always ready to hand, but only to be used in the last extremity.

Molière

If anyone is crazy enough to want to kill a president of the United States, he can do it. All he must be prepared to do is give his life for the president's.

John F. Kennedy

The runaway from trouble is a form of cowardice and, while it is true that the suicide braves death, he does it not for some noble object but to escape some ill.

Aristotle

It was for them to decide. Why live, if living is merely not dying? But to die in order to save one's life, is not that the greatest dupery of all?

Simone de Beauvoir

The man who, in a fit of melancholy, kills himself today would have wished to live had he waited a week.

Voltaire

The question is whether (suicide) is the way out, or the way in.

Ralph Waldo Emerson

Probably no one commits suicide without thinking of it much of his life.

Alfred Kazin

Denial

Everything has been written which could by possibility persuade us that death is not an evil, and the weakest men as well as heroes have given a thousand celebrated examples to support this opinion. Nevertheless, I doubt whether any man of good sense ever believed it.

La Rochefoucauld

No young man believes he shall ever die.

William Hazlitt

Men shun the thought of death as sad, but death will only be sad to those who have not thought of it.

Francis Bacon

As men are not able to fight against death, misery, ignorance, they have taken it into their heads, in order to be happy, not to think of them at all. Despite these miseries, man wishes to be happy, and only wishes to be happy, and cannot wish not to be so. But how will he set about it? To be happy he would have to make himself immortal; but, not being able to do so, it has occured to him to prevent himself from thinking of death.

Blaise Pascal

It astonishes me to observe how irritated moderns become, not so much at the thought as at the mention of death. That's one thing they don't quite know how to take. I don't mean that we should be "brave." That stinks. But it is equally asinine to pretend to ignore it.

William Carlos Williams

Gaily I lived as ease and nature taught,
And I spent my little life without a thought,
And am amazed that Death, that tyrant grim,
Should think of me, who never thought of him.

René F. Regnier

Nature is honest, we aren't; we embalm our dead.

Ugo Betti

Despair

You may give over plow, boys,
You may take the gear to the stead,
All the sweat o' your brow, boys,
Will never get beer and bread.
The seed's waste, I know, boys,
There's not a blade will grow, boys,
'Tis cropped out, I trow, boys,
And Tommy's dead.

Sydney Dobell

I have been all things, and it avails me naught.

Emperor Septimius Severus

And so I leave this world where one's heart either breaks or turns to lead.

S.R.N. Chamfort

When you start thinking of death, you are no longer certain of life.

Hebrew proverb

Few men ever drop dead from overwork, but many quietly curl up and die because of undersatisfaction.

Sidney J. Harris

From the winter's grey despair,
From the summer's golden languor,
Death, the lover of Life,
Frees us for ever.

William E. Henley

What if a man is burried alive every now and then?
For every one of them there are a hundred dead men walking
the earth.

Georg C. Lichtenberg

There are many who dare not kill themselves for fear of what
the neighbours will say.

Cyril Connolly

If one truly has lost hope, one would not be on hand to say so.

Eric Bentley

He is miserable that dieth not before he desires to die.

Thomas B. Fuller

Death is rather to be chosen than a toilsome life, and not to be
born is better than to be born to misery.

Aeschylus

Death is evidently not a real tragedy for those who do not feel life.

Arthur Janov

The naked map of life is spread out before me, and in the emptiness and desolation I see death coming to meet me.

William Hazlitt

I have lived in doubt, I die in anxiety, I know not whither I go.

Anonymous

E

EPITAPHS

Epitaphs

No funeral gloom, my dears, when I am gone,
Corpse-gazings, tears, black raiment, grave-yard grimmes;
Think of me as withdrawn into the dimness,
Yours still, you mine: remember all the best
Of our past moments, and forget the rest;
And so, to where I wait, come gently on.

William Allingham

Speak not evil of the dead, but call them blessed.

Chilo

Epitaph, an inscription on a tomb showing that virtues acquired by death have retroactive effect.

Ambrose Bierce

When a man dies, and his kin are glad of it, they say, "He is better off."

Ed Howe

Remember me when I am gone away,
Gone far away into the silent land.

Christina Rossetti

No longer for me when I am dead
Then you shall hear the surly sullen bell
Give warning to the world that I am fled
From this vile world, with vilest worms to dwell;
Nay, if you read this line, remember not
The hand that writ it; for I love you so
That I in your sweet thoughts would be forgot
If thinking on me then should make you woe.

Shakespeare

Oh! that we two lay sleeping
In our nest in the churchyard sod,
With our limbs at rest on the quiet earth's breast,
And our souls at home with God.

Charles Kingsley

To live a good life; to die a holy death—that is everything.

St. Teresa of Lisieux

Yea, say that I went down to death
  Serene and unafraid,
Still loving Song, but loving more
Life, of which Song is made!

Harry Kemp

The grave is mine house: I have made my bed in the darkness.

The Bible

F

FAREWELLS
FEAR
FILLING THE SHOES
FUNERALS

Farewells

Good-by world . . . Good-by to clocks ticking . . . and Mama's sunflowers. And food and coffee. And new-ironed dresses and hot baths . . . and sleeping and waking up. Oh, earth, you're too wonderful for anybody to realize you.

Thornton Wilder

In every parting there is an image of death.

George Eliot (Mary Ann Evans)

The hour of departure has arrived, and we go our ways—I to die, and you to live. Which is the better, God only knows.

Socrates

I have been dying for twenty years.
Now I am going to live.

James Bruns, dying

I have lived an honest and useful life to mankind: my time has been spent in doing good; and I die in perfect composure and resignation to the will of my Creator.

Thomas Paine

I am perfectly resigned. I am surrounded by my family, I have served my country, I have reliance upon God, and am not afraid of the Devil.

Henry Grattan

───

'Farewell,' says the dying man to his reflection in the mirror that is held up to him, 'we shall not meet again.'

Paul Valéry

───

Farewell my children, forever; I am going to your father.

Marie Antoinette, dying

───

I resign my spirit to God, my daughter to my country.

Thomas Jefferson

───

It is well. I die hard, but am not afraid to go.

George Washington, dying

───

My desire is to make what haste I may to be gone.

Oliver Cromwell, dying

───

I have had my span of life. All I want now is heaven.

Ferdinand Foch, dying

───

I am going to see the sun for the last time.

Jean Jacques Rousseau, dying

This is the last of earth! I am content.

> John Quincy Adams, dying

I leave this world without a regret.

> Henry David Thoreau, dying

Let the tent be struck.

> Robert E. Lee, dying

Put out the light.

> Theodore Roosevelt, dying

I die happy.

> Charles J. Fox, dying

Fear

I am extremely afraid of dying.

> Samuel Johnson

And, to add greater honours to his age
Than man could give him, he died fearing God.

> Shakespeare

Defective piety or love in a dying person is necessarily accompanied by great fear, which is greatest where the piety or love is least. This fear or horror is sufficient in itself, whatever else might be said, to constitute the pain of purgatory.

Martin Luther

The better a man is, the more afraid he is of death.

Samuel Johnson

We can stare in the face neither the sun nor death.

La Rochefoucauld

Men fear Death, as children fear to go in the dark; and as that natural fear in children is increased with tales, so is the other.

Francis Bacon

Fear is an instructor of great sagacity and the herald of all revolutions.

Flannery O'Connor

He who does not fear death has no fear of threats.

Pierre Corneille

The fear of death is the most unjustified of all fears, for there's no risk of accident to someone who's dead.

Albert Einstein

Why, do you now know, then that the origin of all human evils, and of baseness, and cowardice, is not death, but rather the fear of death?

Epictetus

In the depth of the anxiety of having to die is the anxiety of being eternally forgotten.

Paul Tillich

Fear of death is worse than dying.

Johann C. F. von Schiller

The coward fears death and that's all he fears.

Jean Racine

Cowards die many times before their deaths;
The valient never taste of death but once.
Of all the wonders that I yet have heard,
It seems to me most strange that men should fear;
Seeing that death, a necessary end,
Will come when it will come.

Shakespeare

Why be afraid of death
As though your life were breath?
Why should you fear to meet
The Thresher of the wheat?

Maltbie D. Babcock

Far happier are the dead, methinks, than they
Who look for death, and fear it every day.

William Cowper

It is better to die once for all than to live in constant expectation of death.

Julius Caesar

Nay why should I fear Death,
Who gives us life, and in exchange takes breath?

Frederick L. Knowles

That day, which you fear as being the end of all things, is the birthday of your eternity.

Seneca

To die without fear of death is a desirable death.

Seneca

He who fears death cannot enjoy life.

Spanish proverb

When I was analyzing I observed clearly that the fear of death was in proportion to not-living. The less a person was in life, the greater the fear. By being alive I mean living out of all the cells, all the parts of one's self. The cells which are denied become atrophied, like a dead arm, and infect the rest of the body. People living deeply have no fear of death.

Anais Nin

The most rational cure after all for the inordinate fear of death is to set a just value on life.

William Hazlitt

The love of life is at bottom only the fear of death.

Arthur Schopenhauer

Dying is ceasing to be afraid.

William Wycherley

'Feared of dying? Were you 'feared of being born?

Old Farmer's Almanac, 1943

The tragedy of men is that they are men. And when there is food and drink, houses and clothing, peace, security and sanity for all, men will still be scared to death of death.

John Whitting

Who ever really saw anything but horror in the smile of the dead?

Alexander Pope

Filling the Shoes

Two or three have died within the last two twelve months, and so many parts of me have been numbed. One sees a picture, reads an anecdote, starts a casual fancy, and thinks to tell of it to this person in preference to every other—the person is gone whom it would have peculiarly suited. It won't do for another. Every departure destroys a class of sympathies.

Charles Lamb

The next heir is always suspected and disliked.

Tacitus

How sad it is that when a man dies his wisdom, his youth, his beauty, or his virtue cannot be inherited!

Walter Von der Vogelweide

To our graves we walk
In the thick footprint of departed men.

Alexander Smith

When your late husband used to sit in this doorway, he lent dignity and radiance to the whole street. But a house without a husband is worth little.

Juan Ruiz

Those who living fill the smallest space,
In death have often left the greatest void.

Walter S. Landor

You scarce would think so small a thing
    Could leave a loss so large;
Her little light such shadow fling
    From dawn to sunset's marge.
In other springs our life may be
    In bannered bloom unfurled,
But never, never match our wee
    White Rose of all the world.

Gerald Massey

Funerals

A white casket with silver handles, she thought. Not a soft bed with a pink quilt but four sides and a lid that closes. To be shipped like a shoe in a box from this world to the next.

Helen Hudson

Our last garment is made without pockets.

Italian proverb

. . . the city requires a funeral. . . . All the ordinances are designed with your friendly funeral directors in mind—not to mention the cemeteries and coffin makers and gravestone cutters.

Lois Gould

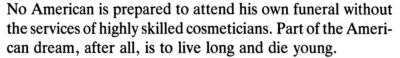

No American is prepared to attend his own funeral without the services of highly skilled cosmeticians. Part of the American dream, after all, is to live long and die young.

Edgar Z. Friedenberg

Funeral, n. A pageant whereby we attest our respect for the dead by enriching the undertaker, and strengthen our grief by an expenditure that deepens our groans and doubles our tears.

Ambrose Bierce

Alas, I am dying beyond my means.

Oscar Wilde

All I desire for my own burial is not to be buried alive.

Lord Chesterfield

Dust to dust, ashes to ashes, and the remains to a memorial park. All this is supposed to maintain the dignity of death. Or is it the dignity of Undertakers?

Joseph W. Krutch

O death where is thy sting? O grave where is thy victory? Where, indeed? Many a badly stung survivor, faced with the aftermath of some relative's funeral, has ruefully conceded that the victory has been won hands down by a funeral establishment—in disastrously unequal battle.

Jessica Mitford

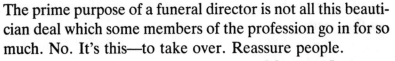

The prime purpose of a funeral director is not all this beautician deal which some members of the profession go in for so much. No. It's this—to take over. Reassure people.

Margaret Laurence

Those who bequeath unto themselves a pompous funeral, are at just so much expense to inform the world of something that has much better be concealed; namely, that their vanity has survived themselves.

Charles C. Colton

Death observes no ceremony.

John Wise

Live so that the preacher can tell the truth at your funeral.

Anonymous

'Tis a good thing funeral sermons are not composed in the confessional.

Finley P. Dunne

All these last offices and ceremonies that concern the dead, the careful funeral arrangements, and the equipment of the tomb, and the pomp of obsequies, are rather the solace of the living than the comfort of the dead.

Saint Augustine of Hippo

A great deal of money is expended on funerals and that, in itself, seems to betray a lack of confidence in the resurrection of the dead.

Edward Henderson

I think funerals are barbaric and miserable. Everything connected with them—the black, the casket, the shiny hearse, the sepulchral tones of the preacher—is destructive to true memory.

Marya Mannes

The pomp of funerals has more regard to the vanity of the living than the honour of the dead.

La Rochefoucauld

When I am dead, no pageant train
   Shall waste their sorrows at my bier,
Nor worthless pomp of homage vain
   Stain it with hypocritic tear.

Edward Everett

GRAVE'S VICTORY
GUILT

Grave's Victory

It costs me never a stab nor squirm
To tread by chance upon a worm.
"Aha, my little dear," I say,
"Your clan will pay me back one day."

Dorothy Parker

Numberless are the world's wonders, but none more wonderful than man . . . from every wind. He has made himself secure—from all but one: In the late wind of death he cannot stand.

Sophocles

If you know not how to die, take no care for it. Nature herself will fully and sufficiently teach you in the proper time, she will exactly discharge that work for you; trouble not yourself with it.

Michel de Montaigne

You may win your heart's desire, but in the end you're cheated of it by death.

Jorge Luis Borges

Six feet of earth makes us all one size.

Italian proverb

The state of man is not unlike that of a fish hooked by an angler. Death allows us a little line. We flounce, and sport, and vary our situation. But when we would extend our schemes, we discover our confinement, checked and limited by a superior hand, who drags us from our element whenever he pleases.

William Shenstone

A beggar on his feet is worth more than an emperor in his grave.

French proverb

There is no king more terrible than death.

Austin Dobson

The bodies of those that made such a noise and tumult when alive, when dead, lie as quietly among the graves of their neighbors as any others.

Jonathan Edwards

The grave is the general meeting-place.

Thomas B. Fuller

Of all events which constitute a person's biography, there is scarcely one . . . to which the world so easily reconciles itself as to his death.

Nathaniel Hawthorne

Then said his servants unto him, What thing is this that thou hast done? thou didst fast and weep for the child, while it was alive; but when the child was dead, thou didst rise and eat bread. And he said, While the child was yet alive, I fasted and wept: for I said, Who can tell whether God will be gracious to me, that the child may live? But now he is dead, wherefore should I fast? can I bring him back again? I shall go to him, but he shall not return to me.

The Bible

His breath goeth forth,
he returneth to his earth;
in that very day his thoughts perish.

The Bible

Such is the frailty of man that even where he makes the truest and most forcible impression—in the memory, in the heart of his beloved,—there also he must perish.

Johann W. von Goethe

Men are carried by horses, fed by cattle, clothed by sheep, defended by dogs, imitated by monkeys, and eaten by worms.

Hungarian proverb

Guilt

When a man thinks himself to be near death, fears and cares enter into his mind which he never had before; the tales of a world below and the punishment which is exacted there of deeds done here were once a laughing matter to him, but now he is tormented with the thought that they may be true: either from the weakness of age, or because he is now drawing nearer to that other place, he has a clearer view of these things; suspicions and alarms crowd thickly upon him, and he begins to reflect and consider what wrongs he has done to others. And when he finds that the sum of his transgressions is great he will many a time like a child start up in his sleep for fear, and he is filled with dark forebodings. But to him who is conscious of no sin, sweet hope . . . is the kind nurse of his age.

Plato

The conscience of the dying man calumniates his life.

Luc de Varvenargues

If there be a pain which devils might pity man for enduring, it is the death-bed reflection that we have possessed the power of doing good, but we have abused and perverted it to the purposes of ill.

Charles C. Colton

Souls in punishment will seek death. They prefer not to be, rather than to be punished. It is for this they shall seek death and not find it. In this sense, every human soul is immortal.

Origen

It would be better to eschew sin than to flee from death.

Thomas à Kempis

When we lose one we love, our bitterest tears are called forth by the memory of hours when we loved not enough.

Maurice Maeterlinck

I remember those happy days and often wish I could speak into the ears of the dead the gratitude which was due to them in life and so ill-returned.

Gwyn Thomas

It is only sudden death we need fear.

Blaise Pascal

The reason why worry kills more people than work is that more people worry than work.

Robert Frost

H

HEALING ALL WOUNDS

HEREAFTERS

HOPE

Healing All Wounds

O eloquent, just, and mighty Death! whom none could advise, thou hast persuaded; what none hath dared, thou hast done; . . . thou hast drawn together all the far-stretched greatness, all the pride, cruelty, and ambition of man, and covered it over with these two narrow words.

Sir Walter Raleigh

Death quits all scores.

James Shirley

Death, the great reconciler.

George Eliot (MaryAnn Evans)

Who can look down upon the grave even of an enemy, and not feel a compunctious throb, that he should ever have warred with the poor handful of earth that lies mouldering before him.

Washington Irving

Death softens all resentments, and the consciousness of a common inheritance of frailty and weakness modifies the severity of judgment.

John Greenleaf Whittier

And, as she looked around, she saw how Death, the consoler,
Laying his hand upon many a heart, had healed it forever.

Henry Wadsworth Longfellow

<hr/>

From out the throng and stress of lies,
From out the painful noise of sighs,
One voice of comfort seems to rise:
"It is the meaner part that dies."

William Morris

<hr/>

The grave unites; where e'en the great find rest,
And blended lie th' oppressor and th' oppressed.

Alexander Pope

<hr/>

Come death, if you will: you cannot divide us; you can only
unite us.

Franz Grillparcer

Hereafters

If you question any candid person who is no longer young, he
is very likely to tell you that, having tasted life in this world,
he has no wish to begin again as a "new boy" in another.

Bertrand Russell

What is death? Either a transition or an end. I am not afraid of coming to an end, this being the same as never having begun, nor of transition, for I shall never be in confinement quite so cramped anywhere else as I am here.

Seneca

The fundamental difference between youth and age will always be that the former has in prospect life, the latter death.

Arthur Schopenhauer

Death is fortunate for the child, bitter to the youth, too late to the old.

Publilius Syrus

Christ's death has impressed the world more than His resurrection.

Paul Valéry

We are today more exercised about life with God on earth than on what will happen to us after . . . death.

Claude G. Montefiore

Death has but one terror—that it has no tomorrow.

Eric Hoffer

We die once, and for such a long time!

Molière

Wherefore, O judges, be of good cheer about death, and know of a certainty, that no evil can happen to a good man, either in life or after death.

Plato

———

Mortality has its compensations; one is that all evils are transitory, another that better times may come.

George Santayana

———

In a way dying is like having children—you never know what will come out.

Joseph Heller

———

To die is different from what any one supposed, and luckier.

Walt Whitman

———

Death is the next step after the pension—it's perpetual retirement without pay.

Jean Giraudoux

———

Let us not lament too much the passing of our friends. They are not dead but simply gone before us along the road which all must travel.

Antiphanes

And as for death, if there be any gods, it is no grevious thing to leave the society of men. The gods will do thee no hurt, thou mayest be sure. But if it be so that there be no gods, or that they take no care of the world, why should I desire to live in a world void of gods, and of all divine providence.

Marcus Aurelius

The world so quickly readjusts itself after any loss, that the return of the departed would nearly always, throw it, even the circle most interested, into confusion.

Charles D. Warner

Actually, I have only two things to worry about now: afterlife and reincarnation.

Gail Parent

What fear of death is like the fear beyond it?

Robert Montgomery

If I stoop: Into a dark tremendous sea of cloud, It is but for a time. I shall emerge one day.

Robert Browning

I know transplanted human worth
Will bloom to profit, otherwhere.

Alfred Lord Tennyson

I trouble not myself about the manner of future existence. I content myself with believing, even to positive conviction, that the power that gave me existence is able to continue it, in any form and manner he pleases, either with or without this body: and it appears more probable to me that I shall continue to exist hereafter than that I should have had existence, as I now have, before that existence began.

Thomas Paine

Death is not anything . . . death is not. . . . It's the absence of presence, nothing more . . . the endless time of never coming back . . . a gap you can't see. And when the wind blows through it, it makes no sound.

Tom Stoppard

Hope

It is plain that the hope of a future life arises from the feeling, which exists in the breast of every man, that the temporal is inadequate to meet and satisfy the demands of his nature.

Immanuel Kant

Old man, exhausted by ordeal, detached from human deeds, feeling the approach of the eternal cold, but always watching the shadows for the gleam of hope.

Charles de Gaulle

Our own death is indeed unimaginable, and whenever we make the attempt to imagine it we can perceive that we really survive as spectators. Hence the psychoanalytic school could venture on the assertion that at bottom no one believes in his own death, or to put the same thing in another way, in the unconscious every one of us is convinced of his immortality.

Sigmund Freud

The man who refuses firmly to entertain the hope of immortality . . . is no more brave and realistic than a man who refuses to open the door of his dark room and come out into the sunshine.

D.G.M. Jackson

A good man has more hope in his death than a wicked man in his life.

Thomas B. Fuller

I have good hope that there is something after death.

Plato

Purgatory is only a throughfare to the Father, toilsome indeed and painful, but yet a throughfare, in which there is no standing still and which is illuminated by glad hope.

Karl Adam

Ah! well! for us all some sweet hope lies
Deeply buried from human eyes;
And, in the hereafter, angels may
Roll the stone from its grave away!

John Greenleaf Whittier

If in the hour of death the conscience is at peace, the mind need not be troubled. The future is full of doubt, indeed, but fuller still of hope.

John Lubbock

No one knows but that death is the greatest of all human blessings.

Plato

There may be little or much beyond the grave,
But the strong are saying nothing until they see.

Robert Frost

Death is the greatest evil, because it cuts off hope.

William Hazlitt

IMMORTALITY
INCH BY INCH
INHERITANCES

Immortality

Still seems it strange, that thou shouldst live forever?
Is it less strange, that thou shouldst live at all?
This is a miracle; and that no more.

Edward Young

Our Creator would never have made such lovely days, and have given us the deep hearts to enjoy them, above and beyond all thought, unless we were meant to be immortal.

Nathaniel Hawthorne

I can easily overlook any present momentary sorrow when I reflect that it is in my power to be happy a thousand years hence. If it were not for this thought I had rather be an oyster than a man.

George Berkeley

Death would be terrifying if there were not alongside it, resplendent immortality.

Adrien-Emanuel Roquette

Surely God would not have created such a being as a man, with an ability to grasp the infinite, to exist only for a day. No, no man was made for immortality.

Abraham Lincoln

When Judaism speaks of immortality. . . its primary meaning is that man contains something independent of the flesh and surviving it, his consciousness and moral capacity, his essential personality, a soul.

Milton Steinberg

Eternity is a terrible thought. I mean, where's it going to end?

Tom Stoppard

Millions long for immortality who do not know what to do with themselves on a rainy Sunday afternoon.

Susan Ertz

Our current obsession with creativity is the result of our continued striving for immortality in an era when most people no longer believe in an after-life.

Arianna Stassinopoulos

If a man can bridge the gap between life and death, if he can live after he's died, maybe then he was a great man. Immortality is the only true success.

Derek Marlowe

There is nothing strictly immortal, but immortality.

Thomas Browne

The carpenter of Galilee, who walked up and down the roads of Palestine two thousand years ago, lived and thought in terms of the immortal. His thoughts were the thoughts of one who was immortal. His talk was the talk of an immortal. He forgave like an immortal. He prayed like an immortal. He died like an immortal, and he lives today as an immortal.

Victor B. Nelson

Oh may I join the choir invisible
Of those immortal dead who live again.

Marian Evans

Inch By Inch

Fog is very terrible. It comes about you before you realize and you are suddenly blind and dumb and cold. It really does seem like death. . . .

Anne Morrow Lindbergh

Each day is a little life: every waking and rising a little birth, every fresh morning a little youth, every going to rest and sleep a little death.

Arthur Schopenhauer

Ah, yet more terrible is the lonely sickbed into which death steals little by little, concealing itself under our covers and behaving so intimately.

Ludwig Tieck

Death takes us piecemeal, not at a gulp.

Seneca

As those we love decay, we die in part;
String after string is severed from the heart.

Francis Thompson

Death stole in like a thief.

Victor Hugo

First our pleasure die—and then
Our hopes, and then our fears—and when
These are dead, the debt is due,
Dust claims dust—and we die too.

Percy Bysshe Shelley

We all do fade as a leaf.

The Bible

When you cease to make a contribution you begin to die.

Eleanor Roosevelt

The lower creation learns death first in the moment of death; man proceeds onward with the knowledge that he is every hour approaching nearer to death, and this throws a feeling of uncertainty over life, even to the man who forgets in busy scenes that annihilation is awaiting him. It is for this reason chiefly that we have philosophies and religions.

Arthur Schopenhauer

When a man dies, he does not just die of the disease he has: he dies of his whole life.

Charles Peguy

The major portion of death has already passed.
Whatever years lie behind us are in death's hands.

Seneca

We do not die wholly at our deaths: we have mouldered away gradually long before. Faculty after faculty, interest after interest, attachment after attachment disappear; we are torn from ourselves while living.

William Hazlitt

I feel so much the continual death of everything and every-body, and have so learned to reconcile myself to it, that the final and official end loses most of its impressiveness.

George Santayana

The little toy dog is covered with dust,
  But sturdy and stanch he stands;
And the little toy soldier is red with rust,
  And his musket moulds in his hands.
Time was when the little toy dog was new,
  And the soldier was passing fair;
And that was the time when our little Boy Blue
  Kissed them and put them there.

Eugene Field

The last hour reaches, but every hour approaches, death.
Death wears us away, but does not whirl us away.

Seneca

So fades a summer cloud away;
  So sinks the gale when storms are o'er;
So gently shuts the eye of day;
  So dies a wave along the shore.

Anna L. Barbauld

So nature deals with us, and takes away
  Our playthings one by one, and by the hand
    Leads us to rest so gently, that we go.

Scarce knowing if we wish to go or stay,
  Being too full of sleep to understand
  How far the unknown transcends the what we know.

Henry Wadsworth Longfellow

Inheritances

Just as I went into politics because Joe died, if anything happened to me tomorrow, Bobby would run for my seat in the Senate. And if Bobby died, our younger brother Teddy would take over for him.

John F. Kennedy

Death is free from Fortune; the earth takes back everything which it has brought forth.

Lucan

Death is a thing of grandeur. It brings instantly into being a whole new network of relations between you and the ideas, the desires, the habits of the man now dead. It is a rearrangement of the world.

Antoine de Saint-Exupéry

After my mother's death I began to see her as she had really been . . . . It was less like losing someone than discovering someone.

Nancy Hale

There is nothing earthly that lasts so well, on the whole, as money. A man's learning dies with him; even his virtues fade out of remembrance, but the dividends on the stocks he bequeaths to his children live and keep his memory green.

Oliver Wendell Holmes

The dead don't die. They look on and help.

D.H. Lawrence

You can leave a will directing how to handle your money, but not your reputation. The public will attend to that.

Bertie Charles Forbes

After their death I only weigh up people by their works.

Voltaire

When it comes to divide an estate, the politest men quarrel.

Ralph Waldo Emerson

The man who leaves money to charity in his will is only giving away what no longer belongs to him.

Voltaire

Death does not always listen to the promises and prayers of those who would inherit.

Molière

When you have told anyone you have left him a legacy, the only decent thing to do is to die at once.

Samuel Butler

Men forget more easily the death of their father than the loss of their patrimony.

Niccolo Machiavelli

JOURNEYS
JUDGMENT DAYS

Journeys

Actually, the process of birth continues. The child begins to recognize outside objects, to react affectively, to grasp things and to coordinate his movements, to walk. But birth continues. The child learns to speak, it learns to know the use and function of things, it learns to relate itself to others, to avoid punishment and gain praise and liking. Slowly, the growing person learns to love, to develop his powers; to acquire a sense of identity, to overcome the seduction of his senses for the sake of an integrated life. . . . The whole life of the individual is nothing but the process of giving birth to himself; indeed, we should be fully born, when we die—although it is the tragic fate of most individuals to die before they are born.

Erich Fromm

Why dost thou fear thy last day? It contributes no more to thy death than does every other day. The last step does not cause the lassitude: it declares it. All days journey towards death; the last arrives there.

Michel de Montaigne

All goes onward and outward, nothing collapses,
And to die is different from what anyone supposed, and
luckier.
Has anyone supposed it lucky to be born?
I hasten to inform him or her it is just as lucky to die, and
know it.

Walt Whitman

Thou carriest them away as with a flood;
   they are as a sleep:
in the morning they are like grass
   which groweth up.
In the morning it flourisheth, and
   groweth up;
in the evening it is cut down, and withereth.

                                        The Bible

———

Life flees and does not pause a single hour—and death, with
great strides, follows close behind.

                              Francesco Petrarca

———

Death is a detail. Death is nothing more than changing gears
in the journey of life.

                              Hubert van Zeller

———

Death is but a name, a date,
A milestone by the stormy road,
Where you may lay aside your load
And bow your face and rest and wait,
Defying fear, defying fate.

                              Joaquim Miller

———

What is your life more than a short day in which the sun
hardly rises before it is lost in the utter darkness of the cold
night?

                     Andres Fernandes de Andrada

I am going to my Father's; and though with great difficulty I have got hither, yet now I do not repent me of all the trouble I have been to arrive where I am. My word I give to him that shall succeed me in my pilgrimage, and my courage and skill to him that can get it. My marks and scars I carry with me to be a witness for me that I have fought His battle who will now be my rewarder.

John Bunyan

Grieve not; though the journey of life be bitter, and the end unseen, there is no road which does not lead to an end.

Hafiz

Death—Life's servitor and friend—the guide
That safely ferries us from shore to shore!

Florence Earle Coates

Death is not the cessation of life, but an incident in it. It is but the "narrows," to use the Psalmist's striking expression, through which the soul passes on its fateful voyage.

Morris Joseph

There is no death! What seems so is transition;
This life of mortal breath
Is but a suburb of the life elysian,
Whose portal we call death.

Henry Wadsworth Longfellow

He left a world he was weary of with the cool indifference you quit a dirty inn, to continue your journey to a place where you hope for better accommodation.

Mary Wortley Montagu

———

So that he seemed to depart not from life, but from one home to another.

Cornelius Nepos

———

I think of death as some delightful journey
That I shall take when all my tasks are done.

Ella Wheeler

———

They are not dead; life's flag is never furled:
They passed from world to world.

Edwin Markham

Judgment Days

Human life, because it is marked by a beginning and an end, becomes whole, an entirety in itself that can be subjected to judgment only when it has ended in death. Death not merely ends life, it also bestows upon it a silent completeness, snatched from the hazardous flux to which all things are subject.

Hannah Arendt

When Death summons a man to appear before his Creator, three friends are his: The first, whom he loves most, is money, but money cannot accompany him one step; his second friend is relatives, but they can only accompany him to the grave, and cannot defend him before the judge. It is his third friend, whom he does not highly esteem, his good deeds, who can go with him, and can appear before the King, and can obtain his acquittal.

The Talmud

Heaven-gates are not so highly arch'd
As prince's palaces; they that enter there
Must go upon their knees.

John Webster

On Judgment Day, God will not ask to what sect you belonged, but what manner of life you led.

I. M. Kagan

At the Day of Judgment it shall not be asked of us what we have read, but what we have done; not how well we have said, but how religiously we have lived.

Thomas à Kempis

Unless we are willing to believe that the Creator and Ruler of the world is unjust, we must believe in a future life wherein He will render to everyone according to his deeds.

Martin J. Scott

In everything else there may be sham: the fine reasonings of philosophy may be a mere pose in us; or else our trials, by not testing us to the quick, give us a chance to keep our face always composed. But in the last scene, between death and ourselves, there is no more pretending; we must talk plain French, we must show what there is that is good and clean at the bottom of the pot.

Michel de Montaigne

On the Day of Judgment, when the trumpets sound, and we are finished with life on earth, we shall be required to justify every word that has carelessly fallen from our lips.

Johann W. von Goethe

It is assumed that a dying man will tell the truth.

Latin proverb

Heaven is not thrown open exclusively to men of heroic calibre.

Edward Leen

The judgment of God shall turn topsy-turvy the judgments of men.

Edward F. Garesche

The thought of death certainly influences the conduct of life less than might have been expected.

John Lubbock

Have pity upon every man, Lord in that hour when he has finished his task and stands before Thee like a child whose hands are being examined.

Paul Claudel

The wicked with the devil will receive eternal punishment while the good with Christ will receive eternal glory.

The Fourth Lateran Council, 1215

May you get to Heaven a half hour before the Devil knows you're dead.

Irish proverb

As there is no other avenue into the world of glory except through death, so there is no entrance into eternal life, except through the narrow pass of judgment.

Emil Brunner

Heaven is above all yet; there sits a judge that no king can corrupt.

Shakespeare

A good life fears not life nor death.

Thomas B. Fuller

L

LAST ACTS
LEFT BEHIND
LIVING LIFE
LONGEVITY
LOVED ONES

Last Acts

A lot of people, on the verge of death, utter famous last words or stiffen into attitudes, as if the final stiffening in three days' time were not enough; they will have ceased to exist three days' hence, yet they still want to arouse admiration and adopt a pose and tell a lie with their last gasp.

Henry de Montherlant

Death is but a little word, but 'tis a great work to die.

Harry Vane, dying

Our life gets as complicated as a comedy as it goes on, but the complications get gradually resolved: see that the curtain comes down on a good denouement.

Gracian

More cruel than death itself was the moment of death.

Pliny The Younger

As I follow some insignificant mortal along the pavement, I am always led to reflect that he, even he, will at some moment be the very centre of the interest of humanity, viz: at the moment of his death.

George Gissing

Suppose that one man should die quietly, another should die suddenly, and a third should die under great consternation of spirit, no man can judge of their eternal condition by the manner of any of these kinds of deaths.

John Bunyan

While eating dinner, this little child,
  Was choked on a piece of beef,
Doctors came, tried their skill awhile,
  But none could give relief.

Julia A. Moore

I have said, Ye are gods. . .
But ye shall die like men.

The Bible

With what strife and pains we come into the world we know not, but 'tis commonly no easy matter to get out of it.

Thomas Browne

Strength or weakness at the hour of death depends on the nature of the last illness.

Luc de Vauvenargues

My father died a difficult and terrible death. It was the first and only time I had seen somebody die. God grants an easy death only to the just.

Svetlana Alliluyeva

If you have served God in a holy life, send away the women and the weepers; . . . and when thou art alone, or with fitting company, die as thou shouldest, but do not die impatiently, and like a fox caught in a trap.

Jeremy Taylor

Is this dying? Is this all? Is this what I feared when I prayed against a hard death? Oh, I can bear this! I can bear it!

Cotton Mather

I imagined it was more difficult to die.

Louis XIV, King of France

How oft when men are at the point of death
They have been merry, which their keepers call
A lightning before death.

Shakespeare

There are two moments in life when every man is respectable—his childhood and his deathbed!

Henri de Montherlant

Death must be distinguished from dying, with which it is often confounded.

Sydney Smith

A good death does honor to a whole life.

Francesco Petrarch

Men die but once, and the opportunity
Of a noble death is not an every day fortune:
It is a gift which noble spirits pray for.

Charles Lamb

I was ever a fighter, so—one fight more,
    The best and the last!
I would hate that death bandaged my eyes, and forbore,
    And bade me creep past.
No! let me taste the whole of it, fare like my peers,
    The heroes of old,
Bear the brunt, in a minute pay glad life's arrears
Of pain, darkness and cold.

Robert Browning

To die well is to die willingly.

Seneca

As it is with a play, so it is with life—what matters is not how
long the acting lasts, but how good it is. It is not important at
what point you stop. Stop wherever you will—only make sure
that you round it off with a good ending.

Seneca

Left Behind

I doubt that we have any right to pity the dead for their own
sakes.

Lord Byron

If I had thought thou couldst have died
  I might not weep for thee;
But I forgot, when by thy side,
  That thou couldnst mortal be;
It never through my mind has past
  The time would e'er be o'er,
And I on thee should look my last,
  And thou shouldst smile no more!

Charles Wolfe

Memorial Service: Farewell party for someone who has already left.

Robert Byrne

What greater pain could mortals have than this:
To see their children dead before their eyes?

Epicurus

To bear, to nurse, to rear,
  To watch and then to lose,
To see my bright ones disappear,
  Drawn up like morning dews.

Jean Ingelow

Oh, call my brother back to me!
  I cannot play alone:
The summer comes with flower and bee,—
  Where is my brother gone?

Felicia Hemans

Hath any loved you well, down there,
    Summer or winter through?
Down there, have you found any fair,
    Laid in the grave with you?
Is death's long kiss a richer kiss
    Than mine was wont to be—
Or have you gone to some far bliss
    And quite forgotten me?

                                Arthur O'Shaughnessy

━━━━━━

He hated her for the selfishness of her death and for her
having eclipsed him forever, obliterated him as if she had
smashed an insect under her shoe.

                                Joyce Carol Oates

━━━━━━

Where shall I follow you? Your corpse defiled, your mangled
limb—where are they?

                                Virgil

━━━━━━

What is the world to a man when his wife is a widow.

                                Irish proverb

━━━━━━

After my husband died, I felt like one of those spiraled shells
washed up on the beach . . . no flesh, no life. . . . We add
ourselves to our men, we exist in their reflection. And then?
If they die?

                                Lynn Caine

Our society is set up so that most women lose their identities when their husbands die. . . . It's wrenching enough to lose the man who is your lover, your companion, your best friend, the father of your children, without losing yourself as well.

Lynn Caine

Can anyone understand how it is to have lived in the White House, and then, suddenly, to be living alone as the President's widow?

Jacqueline Bouvier Kennedy Onassis

"Widow" is a harsh and hurtful word. It comes from the Sanskrit and it means "empty." I have been empty too long.

Lynn Caine

He first deceased; she for little tried
To live without him, liked it not, and died.

Henry Wotton

Living Life

There is no cure for birth and death save to enjoy the interval.

George Santayana

You will die not because you're ill, but because you're alive.

Seneca

When I am dead, forget me, dear,
  For I shall never know.
Though o'er my cold and lifeless hands
  Your burning tears shall flow:
I'll cancel with my living voice
  The debt you owe the dead—
Give me the love you'd show me then,
  But give it now instead.

Celia Congreve

I see clearly that there are two deaths: to cease loving and being loved is unbearable. But to cease to live is of no consequence.

Voltaire

Until death, it is all life.

Cervantes

. . .you don't get to choose how you're going to die. Or when. You can only decide how you're going to live. Now.

Joan Baez

What is so far in life, is too near to death.

Friedrich Hebbel

Dying is easy work compared with living.
Dying is a moment's transition; living a transaction of years.

Maltbie D. Babcock

Most men eddy about,
Here and there—eat and drink,
Chatter and love and hate,
Gather and squander, are raised
Aloft, are hurled in the dust,
Striving blindly, achieving
Nothing; and then they die—
Perish;—and no one asks
Who or what they have been.

Matthew Arnold

If I were a writer of books I would compile a register, with a commentary, of the different deaths that men die, for he who would teach them how to die would also teach them how to live.

Michel de Montaigne

It matter not how a man dies, but how he lives.

Samuel Johnson

Neither dread your last day nor desire it.

Marcus Valerius Martial

To achieve great things, we must live as though we were never going to die.

Luc de Vauvenargues

The eternal gods are ever full of life; but man too can also keep in mind the best he remembers, and thus experience the utmost right up to the time of his death.

Friedrich Holderlin

I gave my life to learning how to live.
Now that I have organized it all . . . . It is just about over.

Sandra Hochman

Life is the childhood of immortality.

Daniel A. Poling

The fundamental thing behind all motivation and all activity is the constant struggle against annihilation and against death.

Woody Allen

I postpone death by living, by suffering, by error, by risking, by giving, by losing.

Anais Nin

I'm the one that's got to die when it's time for me to die, so let me live my life the way I want to.

Jimi Hendrix

Longevity

Old men's prayers for death are lying prayers, in which they abuse old age and long extent of life. But when death draws near, not one is willing to die, and age no longer is a burden to them.

Euripides

The long habit of living indisposeth us for dying.

Thomas Browne

Make sure to send a lazy man for the Angel of Death.

Jewish proverb

I shall mourn my death now, and lament my life since it has been prolonged for my sins.

Saint John of the Cross

As soon as man, expert from time, has found
The key of life, it opens the gates of death.

Edward Young

By medicine life may be prolonged, yet death will seize the doctor too.

Shakespeare

When true hearts lie wither'd
  And fond ones are flown,
Oh, who would inhabit
  This bleak world alone?

Thomas Moore

Old age is an island surrounded by death.

Juan Montalvo

I cannot forgive my friends for dying: I do not find these vanishing acts of theirs at all amusing.

Logan P. Smith

All, all are gone, the old familiar faces.

Charles Lamb

I have not lived eighty years without learning how to stand dying for a quarter of an hour.

The Constable de Montmorenci

Loved Ones

There exists scarcely any man so accomplished, or so necessary to his own family, but he has some failing which will diminish their regret at his loss.

Jean de La Bruyère

On parent knees, a naked new-born child,
Weeping thou sat'st while around thee smiled;
So live, that, sinking to thy life's last sleep,
Calm thou may'st smile, while all around thee weep.

William Jones

At the funerals of our relations we do our best to put on long
faces, but at the luncheon afterwards our hilarity breaks out.
For it is he who has died and not ourselves.

Gerald Brenan

I never wanted to see anybody die, but there are a few
obituary notices I have read with pleasure.

Clarence Darrow

The dead and the absent have no friends.

Spanish proverb

I hate funerals, and would not attend my own if it could be
avoided, but it is well for every man to stop once in a while to
think of what sort of a collection of mourners he is training for
his final event.

Robert T. Morris

I saw a dead man's finer part
Shining within each faithful heart
Of those bereft. Then said I, "This must be
His immortality."

Thomas Hardy

Death never takes one alone, but two!
Whenever he enters in at a door,
Under roof of god or roof of thatch,
He always leaves it upon the latch,
And comes again ere the year is o'er.
Never one of a household only!

Henry Wadsworth Longfellow

Clasp my hand, dear friend, I am dying.

Vittorio Alfieri, dying

What the mother sings to the cradle goes all the way down to
the coffin.

Henry Ward Beecher

With more fortitude does a mother mourn one out of many,
than she who weeping cries, "Thou wert my only one."

Ovid

Love is the only effective counter to death.

Maureen Duffy

They that love beyond the world, cannot be separated. Death cannot kill what never dies. Nor can Spirits ever be divided that love and live in the same Divine Principle; the Root and Record of their Friendship. Death is but crossing the world, as Friends do the Seas; they live in one another still.

William Penn

The sorrow for the dead is the only sorrow from which we refuse to be divorced. . . . The love which survives the tomb is one of the noblest attributes of the soul.

Washington Irving

M

MAKING THE BEST OF IT
MEETING YOUR MAKER
MONUMENTS
MOURNERS
MYSTERIES

Making The Best of It

When the cancer that later took his life was first diagnosed, Senator Richard L. Newberger remarked upon his "new appreciation of things I once took for granted—eating lunch with a friend, scratching my cat Muffet's ears and listening for his purrs, the company of my wife, reading a book or magazine in the quiet of my bed lamp at night, raiding the refrigerator for a glass of orange juice or a slice of toast. For the first time, I think I actually am savoring life."

Richard L. Newberger

Life is a terrifying experience, but oblivion is sadder.

Tennessee Williams

The soul in purgatory feels great happiness and great sorrow, and the one does not hinder the other.

Saint Catherine of Genoa

All men should strive to learn before they die what they are running from, and to, and why.

James Thurber

Verily, verily, I say unto you, Except a corn of wheat fall into the ground and die, it abideth alone: but if it die, it bringeth forth much fruit. He that loveth his life shall lose it; and he that hateth his life in this world shall keep it unto life eternal.

The Bible

And I will show that there is no imperfection in the
present, and can be none in the future,
And I will show that whatever happens to anybody it
may be turn'd to beautiful results.
And I will show that nothing can happen more beautiful
than death.

Walt Whitman

We're living in a butcher shop. The fact that we die is the only comfort in the whole thing.

Leonard Cohen

Every man should be cheerful and glad, even till he suffers death.

Sayings of the High One
(Old Norse)

It is not a question of dying earlier or later, but of dying well or ill. And dying well means escape from the danger of living ill.

Seneca

The art of living well and the art of dying well are one.

Epicurus

Try not to take life too seriously,
You're not going to get out of it alive anyway.

Carl Douglas

If die you must, then live beforehand, be mine in the spring-time of God's earth.

Henrik Ibsen

Be happy while y'er leevin, for y'er a lang time dead.

Scottish proverb

Let us eat and drink; for tomorrow we shall die.

The Bible

Meeting Your Maker

There is no confessor like unto Death!
Thou canst not see him, but he is near:
Thou needst not whisper above thy breath,
And he will hear.

Henry Wadsworth Longfellow

We must die! These words are hard, but they are followed by a great happiness: it is in order to be with God that we die.

Saint Francis of Sales

All is ashes, phantoms, shadows, smoke—everything will vanish like the dust of a whirlwind, and we shall stand before death unarmed and helpless.

Aleksei Tolstoy

Death is the enlightener. The essential thing concerning it must be that it opens the closed eyes, draws down the veil of blinding mortality, and lets the man see spiritual things.

Phillips Brooks

I am the Dark Cavalier; I am the Last Lover:
My arms shall welcome you when other arms are tired.

Margaret Widdemer

It is to death life owes its seriousness. A life which ended in nothingness would have nothing serious about it . . . would be a game.

Jacques Leclerc

When we come to realize that death that crushes is but the tender clasp of God that loves, it loses all its terror.

Vincent McNabb

What is this world? A dream within a dream as we grow older each step is an awakening. The Grave the last sleep?—no; it is the last and final awakening.

Walter Scott

Death's but a path that must be trod,
If man would ever pass to God.

Thomas Parnell

A man seated in a glass cage is not put to such embarrassment as is a man in his transparency before God. . . . Substantially everyone arrives in eternity bringing with him and delivering the most accurate account of every least insignificance which he has committed or left undone.

Sören Kierkegaard

The first sign of love to God is not to be afraid of death, and to be always waiting for it. For death unites the friend to his friend—the seeker to the object which he seeks.

Al-Ghazzali

What great God is this, that pulls down the strength of the strongest Kings?

Clotaire I

What else, indeed is the judgment, as far as we can grasp it, but the naked setting of our soul as it is now at this moment in the sight of God?

Bede Jarrett

Only of this I am assured, that some time in some way, spirit to spirit, face to face, I shall meet the great Lord of life, and, falling before Him, tell my gratitude for all He has done, and implore pardon for all He has done, and implore pardon for all that I have left undone.

Paul E. More

In no state is there so paradoxical a combination of suffering and joy. For the soul will sufficiently "see" God to realize its own unlikeness to Him. His beauty and its ugliness. . . .But also, it knows that it is becoming more and more like to God, and in that is a joy far greater than any we experience here.

Cyril C. Martindale

One is born amongst men; one dies, unconsoled, among the gods.

René Char

When on my sick-bed I languish,
Full of sorrow, full of anguish
Fainting, gasping, trembling, crying,
Panting, groaning, speechless, dying, . . .
Methinks I hear some gentle spirit say,
Be not fearful, come away.

Thomas Flatman

Here in this world He bids us come, there in the next He shall bid us welcome.

John Donne

I shall rise from the dead, from the dark station, from the prostration, from the prosternation of death, and never miss the sun, which shall then be put out, for I shall see the Son of God, the Sun of glory, and shine myself, as that sun shines.

John Donne

For tho' from out our bourne of time and place
The flood may bear me far,
I hope to see my Pilot face to face
When I have crossed the bar.

Alfred Lord Tennyson

Glory comes at the end, not at the beginning of life.

Lodovico Degli Arrighi

Monuments

Toward the person who has died we adopt a special attitude:
something like admiration for someone who has accomplished
a very difficult task.

Sigmund Freud

The whole earth is a sepulchre for famous men.

Thucydides

Of all the pulpits from which the human voice is ever sent
forth there is none from which it reaches so far as from the
grave.

John Ruskin

Antiquity makes everything more impressive after death. One's name comes grandly into men's mouths once the funeral is over.

Propertius

Men are convinced of your arguments, your sincerity, and the seriousness of your efforts only by your death.

Albert Camus

Time magnifies everything after death; a man's fame is increased as it passes from mouth to mouth after his funeral.

Propertius

A dead man who never caused others to die seldom rates a statue.

Anonymous

If a man was great while living, he becomes tenfold greater when dead.

Thomas Carlyle

Since it is not granted us to live long, let us transmit to posterity some memorial that we have at least lived.

Pliny The Younger

Our bones lie hidden in the grave, but not the memory of our good deeds.

Awang Sulong (Malay)

There, in that manufactured park with its ghoulish artificiality, with its interminable monuments to bad taste, wealth and social position, we were planning to place the body of a beautiful and dignified old man who had lived generously and loved beauty.

Frances Newton

Posthumous charities are the very essence of selfishness when bequeathed by those who, when alive, would part with nothing.

Charles C. Colton

Men use one another to assure their personal victory over death.

Ernest Becker

If fame is to come only after death, I am in no hurry for it.

Marcus Valerius Martial

You are only a legend when you are dead.

Elizabeth Taylor

The strong walled houses of the dead are the ones to have outlived the centuries, not the houses of the living: not the inns of the living, but the dwellings of permanence.

Miguel De Unamuno

You may go now, and hide the dead in his poor tomb; He has those flowers that are the right of the underworld. I think it makes small difference to the dead, if they are buried in the tokens of luxury. All this is an empty glorification left for those who live.

Euripides

Man grows old, and swindles, and decays,
And countless generations of mankind
Depart, and leave no vestige where they trod.

William Wordsworth

After I am dead, I would rather have men ask why Cato has no monument than why he had one.

Cato the Elder

I don't want to own anything that won't fit into my coffin.

Fred Allen

Mourners

Blessed are they that mourn: for they shall be comforted.

The Bible

There are not ten people in the world whose death would spoil my dinner, but there are one or two whose deaths would break my heart.

Thomas B. Macaulay

She lived unknown and few could know
    When Lucy ceased to be:
But she is in her grave, and oh,
    The difference to me!

William Wordsworth

The chief mourner does not always attend the funeral.

Ralph Waldo Emerson

Since every death diminishes us a little, we grieve—not so much for the death as for ourselves.

Lynn Caine

There is a kind of contempt of the landscape felt by him who has just lost by death a dear friend. The sky is less grand as it sets down over less worth in the population.

Ralph Waldo Emerson

I long for household voices gone.

John Greenleaf Whittier

"Weep not," ye mourners, for the dead,
But in this hope spirits soar,
That ye can say of those ye mourn,
They are not lost, but gone before.

Alexander Pope

But when the great and good depart,
What is it more than this—
The Man, who is from God sent forth,
Doth yet again to God return,—
Such ebb and flow must ever be,
Then wherefore should we mourn?

William Wordsworth

One of the chores of grief involves going over and over in one's mind the circumstances that led to the death, the details of the death itself.

Lynn Caine

Ah, my children, you cannot cry for me as much as I have made you laugh.

Paul Scarron, dying

Do not mourn over dying things: look to the east, give your heart to the future. The trees have fallen, but the shoots remain. Reach out your arms to bless those yet to be born.

Victor de Laprade

In time, I hope and believe the anguish with you will be covered over. That is the only way to express it. It is like new skin covering a wound. That doesn't mean that one forgets the people who have gone away.

Edith Stilwell

The dead to their graves, the living to their dinners.

Spanish proverb

――――――

Weep ye not for the dead, neither bemoan him.

The Bible

――――――

Let not the eyes be dry when we have lost a friend, nor let them overflow. We may weep, but we must not wail.

Seneca

――――――

To weep excessively for the dead is to affront the living.

Thomas B. Fuller

――――――

Moderate lamentation is the right of the dead; excessive grief the enemy to the living.

Shakespeare

――――――

There is a limit to the time mourning must be worn, but my tears at least will never leave me.

Mitsinobu

――――――

Let mourning stop when one's grief is fully expressed.

Confucius

Mysteries

The event of death is always astounding; our philosophy never reaches, never possesses it; we are always at the beginning of our catechism; always the definition is yet to be made. What is death?

Ralph Waldo Emerson

Death speaks to us with a deep voice but has nothing to say.

Paul Valéry

Dear, beauteous death, the jewel of the just!
   Shining nowhere but in the dark;
What mysteries do lie beyond thy dust,
   Could man outlook that mark!

Henry Vaughan

We know nothing of this journey that no-one shares with us. We have no reason to look on death with admiration, love or hate; since a masked mouth strangely distorts it with tragic lamentations.

Rainer Maria Rilke

Least of all do I know this very death whose grasp I cannot avoid.

Blaise Pascal

Only music can speak of death.

André Malraux

But that dread of something after death.
The undiscover'd country from whose bourn
No traveller returns, puzzles the will
And makes us rather bear those ills we have
Than fly to others that we know not of?
Thus conscience does make cowards of us all;
And thus the native hue of resolution
Is sicklied o'er with the pale cast of thought.

Shakespeare

When our parents are living we feel that they stand between us and death; when they go, we move to the edge of the unknown.

R.I. Fitzhenry

Death is not an event in life; we do not experience death.

Ludwig Wittgenstein

Life is a great surprise. I do not see why death should not be an even greater one.

Vladimir Nabokov

Know, beloved that we cannot understand the future world until we know what death is; and we cannot know what death is until we know what life is; nor can we understand what life is until we know what the spirit is—the seat of the knowledge of God.

Al-Ghazzali

N

NIRVANA

NO FAVORITES

NO GHOSTS

Nirvana

Death is simply a shedding of the physical body, like the butterfly coming out of a cocoon. It is a transition into a higher state of consciousness, where you continue to perceive, to understand, to laugh, to be able to grow, and the only thing you lose is something that you don't need anymore . . . your physical body. It's like putting away your winter coat when spring comes.

Elisabeth Kubler-Ross

Some people are born again; evil doers go to hell; righteous people go to heaven; those who are free from all worldly desires attain Nirvana.

Dhammapada

The noble Soul in old age returns to God as to that port whence she set forth on the sea of this life. And as the good mariner, when he approaches port, furls his sails . . . so should we furl the sails of our worldly affairs and turn to God with our whole mind and heart, so that we may arrive at the port with all sweetness and peace.

Dante

After the end of this world every nature, whether corporal or incorporal, will seem to be only God, the integrity of the nature remaining, so that God, who is in himself incomprehensible, will be somehow comprehended in the creature.

Johannes Scotus Erigena

As rivers flow into the sea and in so doing lose name and form, even so the wise man, freed from name and form, attains the Supreme being, The Self-luminous, the Infinite.

Mundaka Upanishad

To save life it must be destroyed. When utterly destroyed, one dwells for the first time in peace.

Zenrin Kushu

When the soul returns into itself and reflects, it passes into . . . the region of that which is pure and everlasting, immortal and unchangeable.

Plato

The fever called ''living''
Is conquered at last.

Edgar Allen Poe

No Favorites

What man is he that liveth, and shall not see death?

The Bible

Rome can issue no dispensation from death.

Molière

When death comes, he respects neither age nor merit. He sweeps from this earthly existence the sick and the strong, the rich and the poor, and should teach us to live to be prepared for death.

Andrew Jackson

Death is stronger than all the governments because the governments are men and men die and then death laughs: now you see 'em now you don't.

Carl Sandburg

Death holds no horrors. It is simply the ultimate horror of life.

Jean Giraudoux

One event happeneth to them all.

The Bible

If some persons died, and others did not die, death would indeed be a terrible affliction.

Jean de La Bruyère

Sleep does make us all equal, it seems to me, like his big brother—Death.

Arthur Schinitzler

In the democracy of the dead, all men are equal. The poor man is as rich as the richest, and the rich man as poor as the pauper. The creditor loses his usury, and the debtor is acquitted of his obligation. There the proud man surrenders his dignity; the politician his honors; the worldling his pleasures; the invalid needs no physician; the laborer rests from toil. The wrongs of time are redressed; injustice is expiated, and the irony of fate is refuted.

Anonymous

He who must die must die in the dark, even though he sells candles.

Colombian proverb

Here (on earth) one may be lower than another in honor, and yet the highest want glory: there, though one star differs from another in glory, they all shine as stars. Here the greatest must want—there the least hath enough. Here all the earth may not be enough for one—there one heaven is enough for all.

Arthur Warwick

Death, the only immortal who treats us all alike, whose pity and whose peace and whose refuge are for all—the soiled and the pure, the rich and the poor, the loved and the unloved.

Mark Twain (Samuel Clemens)

As men, we are all equal in the presence of death.

Publilius Syrus

146

The prince, who kept the world in awe,
The judge, whose dictate fix'd the law,
The rich, the poor, the great, the small,
Are levell'd: death confounds 'em all.

John Gay

Death knocks impartially at the door of the poor man's shop and the prince's palace.

Horace

Death levels master and slave, the sceptre and the law, and makes unlike like.

Walter Colman

How dieth the wise man? As the fool.

The Bible

Death is, after all, the only universal experience except birth.

Stewart Alsop

A piece of a churchyard fits everybody.

George Herbert

No Ghosts

Ah, Christ, that it were possible
For one short hour to see
The souls we loved, that they might tell us
What and where they be!

Alfred Lord Tennyson

Who e'er returned to teach the Truth, the things of Heaven
   and Hell to limn?
And all we hear is only fit for grandam-talk and nursery-hymn.

Richard Burton

There is no return to life from death.

Euripides

Man dieth, and wasteth away: yea, man giveth up the ghost,
and where is he?

The Bible

And not a man appears to tell their fate.

Homer

He that goeth down to the grave shall come up no more.

The Bible

Strange, it is not? that of the myriads who
Before us passed the door or Darkness through,
Not one return to tell us of the Road,
Which to discover we must travel too.

Omar Khayyam

The dead do not know what is doing here, but afterward they
hear of it from those who meet them in death.

Saint Augustine of Hippo

And the stately ships go on,
   To their haven under the hill;
But O for the touch of a vanished hand,
   And the sound of a voice that is still!

Alfred Lord Tennyson

From the voiceless lips of the unreplying dead there comes no
word; but in the night of death hope sees a star, and listening
love can hear the rustle of a wing.

Robert C. Ingersoll

OLD AGE
OUT WITH A BANG
OUT WITH A WHIMPER

Old Age

What a poor dotard must he be who has not learnt in the course of so long a life that death is not a thing to be feared? Death, that is either to be totally disregarded, if it entirely extinguishes the soul, or is even to be desired, if it brings him where he is to exist forever. A third alternative, at any rate, cannot possibly be discovered. When then should I be afraid if I am destined either not to be miserable after death or even to be happy? After all, who is such a fool as to feel certain—however young he may be—that he will be alive in the evening? Nay, that time of life has many more chances of death than ours. Young men more easily contract diseases; their illnesses are more serious; their treatment has to be more severe. Accordingly, only a few arrive at old age. If that were not so, life would be conducted better and more wisely; for it is in old men that thought, reason, and prudence are to be found; and if there had been no old men, states would never have existed at all.

Cicero

One thing is sure, there are just two respectable ways to die. One is of old age, and the other is by accident.

Elbert Hubbard

I see myself now at the end of my journey; my toilsome days ended. I am going now to see that head that was crowned with thorns, and that face that was spit upon for me.

John Bunyan

. . . it is old age, rather than death, that is to be contrasted with life. Old age is life's parody, whereas death transforms life into a destiny: in a way it preserves it by giving it the absolute dimension—"As into himself eternity changes him at last." Death does away with time.

Simone de Beauvoir

I must arrange my pillows for another weary night.

Washington Irving, dying

I am so far resigned to my lot that I feel small pain at the thought of having to part from what has been called the pleasant habit of existence . . . I would not care to live my wasted life over again . . . let me slip away as quietly and comfortably as I can.

Frederick L. Lampson

Perhaps nature wants us, at the end of our days, to be disgusted with life, so that we may leave this world with less regret.

Frederick The Great

My life has run his compass.

Shakespeare

The mode of death is sadder than death itself.

Marcus Valerius Martial

Always observe how ephemeral and worthless human things are. . . . Pass then through this little space of time conformably to nature, and end thy journey in content, just as an olive falls off when it is ripe, blessing nature who produced it, and thanking the tree on which it grew.

Marcus Aurelius

Old men must die; or the world would grow
Moldy, would only breed the past again.

Alfred Lord Tennyson

Thou shalt come to thy grave in a full age, like as a shock of corn cometh in in his season.

The Bible

A dying man needs to die, as a sleepy man needs to sleep, and there comes a time when it is wrong, as well as useless, to resist.

Stewart Alsop

When the lessons of life are all ended,
    And death says: "The school is dismissed!"
May the little ones gather around me
    To bid me good night and be kissed.

Charles M. Dickinson

Why shed tears that thou must die? For if thy past life has been one of enjoyment, and if all thy pleasures have not passed through thy mind, as through a sieve, and vanished, leaving not a rack behind, why when dost thou not, like a thankful guest, rise cheerfully from life's feast, and with a quiet mind go take thy rest?

Lucretius

After sixty years the stern sentence of the burial service seems to have a meaning that one did not notice in former years. There begins to be something personal about it.

Oliver Wendell Holmes

Sooner or later I'm going to die, but I'm not going to retire.

Margaret Mead

The end is come of pleasant places,
The end of tender words and faces,
The end of all, the poppied sleep.

Algernon C. Swinburne

Death, kind Nature's signal of retreat.

Samuel Johnson

Out With A Bang

Come to the bridal-chamber, Death!
  Come to the mother's, when she feels,
For the first time, her first-born's breath! . . .
Come when the heart beats high and warm
With banquet-song, and dance, and wine,
And thou art terrible.

Fitz-Greene Halleck

A sudden death is but a sudden joy, if it takes a man in the state and exercise of virtue.

Jeremy Taylor

Happy he who dies before he calls for death to take him away.

Francis Bacon

Some men die early and are spared much care,
  Some suddenly, escaping worse than death;
But he is fortune who happens where
  He can exult and die in the same breath.

Louise Driscoll

Who dies in youth in vigour, dies the best,
Struck thro' with wounds, all honest on the breast.

Homer

Is it not better at an early hour
  In its calm cell to rest the weary head,
While birds are singing and while blooms the bower,
  Than sit the fire out and go starved to bed?

                     Walter S. Landor

A man sometimes shows in his death that he is worthy of living.

                     Francis Ponce

We are reminded how glorious it is to die with sword in hand.

                     Virgil

Better a thousand times to die with glory than live without honor.

                     Louis VI, King of France

Grieve not that I die young. Is it not well
To pass away ere life hath lost its brightness?

                     Flora E. Hastings

Only when a man's life comes to its end in prosperity dare we pronounce him happy.

                     Aeschylus

It is better to die, since death comes surely,
In the full noon-tide of an honored name,
Than to lie at the end of years obscurely,
A handful of dust in a shroud of shame.

James J. Roche

There is a great difference between going oft in warm blood
like Romeo, and making one's exit like a frog in a frost.

John Keats

And could we choose the time and choose aright,
'Tis best to die, our honour at the height.

John Dryden

To die is easy when we are in perfect health. On a fine spring
morning, out of doors, on the downs, mind and body sound
and exhilarated, it would be nothing to lie down on the turf
and pass away.

Mark Rutherford

She died in beauty, like a rose
Blown from its parent stem.

C.D. Sillery

Out With A Whimper

He died, as erring man should die,
Without display, without parade;
Meekly had he bowed and prayed,
As not disdaining priestly aid,
Nor desperate of all hope on high.

Lord Byron

The rose withers, the blossom blasteth,
The flower fades, the morning hasteth,
The sun sets, the shadow flies,
The gourd consumes; and man he dies.

Anonymous

Death does not come with a trumpet.

Danish proverb

He got in like a fox, played the pontiff like a lion, and went
out like a dog.

Epitaph for Pope Boniface VIII

Once we were champions; now we are but dust and shadows.

Ausonius

At last he came, the messenger,
The messenger from unseen lands:
And what did dainty Baby Bell?
She only crossed her little hands,
She only looked more meek and fair!
We parted back her silken hair,
We wove the roses round her brow—
White buds, the summer's drifted snow—
Wrapped her from head to foot in flower. . .
And thus went dainty Baby Bell
Out of this world of ours.

                                    Thomas B. Aldrich

———

The day of death is when two worlds meet with a kiss: this
world going out, the future world coming in.

                                    José B. Abin

———

We watch'd her breathing thro' the night,
   Her breathing soft and low,
As in her breast the wave of life
Kept heaving to and fro. . . .

Our very hopes belied our fears,
   Our fears our hopes belied;
We thought her dying when she slept,
   And sleeping when she died.

                                    Thomas Hood

Then fell upon the house a sudden gloom,
A shadow on those features fair and thin;
And softly, from the hushed and darkened room,
Two angels issued, where but one went in.

Henry Wadsworth Longfellow

To live, to have so much ambition, to suffer, to cry, to fight
and, at the end, forgetfulness . . . as if I had never existed.

Marie Bashkirtsev

For him who has faith, death so far as it is his own death,
ceases to possess any quality of terror. The experiment will be
over, the rinsed beaker returned to its shelf, the crystals gone
dissolving down the wastepipe; the duster sweeps the bench.

H.G. Wells

The end of all is death, and man's life passeth away suddenly
as a shadow.

Thomas à Kempis

How can death be evil, when in its presence we are not aware
of it?

Diogenes

P

PARADISE
PRAYERS
PREPARATION
PROMISED LAND

Paradise

It cannot be that our life is a mere bubble cast up by eternity to float a moment on its waves and then sink into nothingness. Else why is it that the glorious aspirations which leap like angels from the temple of our heart are forever wandering unsatisfied. . . . There is a realm where the rainbow never fades; where the stars will be spread out before us like islands that slumber in the ocean, and where the beautiful beings which now pass before us like shadows will stay in our presence forever.

George D. Prentice

Heaven possesses all light, all goodness, all glory, all fragrance, all joy. . . . It is devoid of want, pain, distress, discomfort . . . the radiance and brightness of the souls in heaven are like the stars and the moon, and they sit on golden thrones . . . and their state of happiness continues up to the day of resurrection.

M.N. Dhalla

In the heaven-world there is no fear; thou art not there, O Death, and no one is afraid on account of old age. Leaving behind both hunger and thirst, and out of the reach of sorrow, all rejoice in the world of heaven.

Katha Upanishad

Surely there must be some place where the great minds of Shelley, Homer and Spinoza go after death. The denial of immortality does not square with intelligence. Adolph S. Ochs, shortly before his death, said that he believed that he was more than an animal and that he did not believe that this life is the end. Our bodies change and in the end crumble. It is a house of clay. But inside there is a spiritual duplicate. As we have borne the image of the earthly, so shall we bear the image of the heavenly.

Malcolm J. MacLeod

When faith and love which parted from thee never,
Had ripened thy just soul to dwell with God;
Meekly thou didst resign this earthly load
Of death called life; which us from life doth sever.
Thy works, and alms, and all thy good endeavour,
Stayed not behind, nor in the grave were trod;
But, as Faith pointed with her golden rod,
Followed thee up to joy and bliss for ever.

John Milton

Passed on, beyond our mortal vision,
But now the thought is robbed of gloom,
Within the Father's many mansions
Still dwelling in another room.

The one whose going left us lonely
Is scaling heights undreamed of yore,
And guided on by Love's unfolding
Has gone upstairs and shut the door.

Anonymous

Fast as the rolling seasons bring
The hour of fate to those we love,
Each pearl that leaves the broken string
Is set in Friendship crown above.
As narrower grows the earthly chain,
The circle widens in the sky;
These are our treasures that remain,
But those are stars that beam on high.

Oliver Wendell Holmes

At going out, we think, and enter straight
Another golden chamber of the king's,
Larger than this we leave, and lovelier.

Philip J. Bailey

The great souls of departed saints, look ever down on earth, and are full of beauty, shining each in its own place, and with its own glory. Saints, and heroes who died in battle, wise kings, and hermits, were there, visible by thousands, angels by thousands, heavenly singers, like to the sun in glory.

Mahabharata

The righteous in Heaven are undecaying and immortal, unharmed, undistressed and undisturbed. Everywhere, they are full of glory, fragrant and joyful, full of delight and full of happiness.

Zend-Avesta

God shall wipe away all tears from their eyes; and there shall be no more death, neither sorrow, no crying, neither shall there be any more pain; for the former things are passed away.

The Bible

Who knows but on their sleep may rise
Such light as never heaven let through
To lighten earth from Paradise?

Algernon C. Swinburne

As a navigator who suddenly disembarks from the cold, wintry and lonely sea, upon a coast which is laden with the warm rich blossoms of spring, so with one leap from our little bark we pass at once from winter to eternal springtime.

Jean Paul Richter

I go from a corruptible to an incorruptible crown, where no disturbance can have place.

Charles I, King of England

As I draw near the borderland . . . the wonderful light of the other life seems often to shine so joyfully into this one, that I almost forget the past and present, in an eager anticipation of the approaching awakening.

Elizabeth Blackwell

There is no death! the stars go down
   To rise upon some other shore,
And bright in Heaven's jeweled crown,
   They shine forevermore.

John L. McCreary

The world recedes; it disappears;
Heav'n opens on my eyes; my ears
   With sounds seraphic ring:
Lend, lend your wings! I mount! I fly!
O Grave! where is thy victory?
   O Death! where is thy sting?

Alexander Pope

The dead have no tears, and forget all sorrow.

Euripides

In death shall I be alone!

German Folksong

Prayers

Absence and death, how differ they? and how
Shall I admit that nothing can restore
What one short sigh so easily removed?
Death, life, and sleep, reality and thought—
Assist me, God, Their boundaries to know,
O teach me calm submission to thy Will!

William Wordsworth

When outward bound we boldly sail
  And leave the friendly shore,
Let not our hearts of courage fail
  Before the voyage is o'er.
We trust in Thee, whate'er befall;
Thy sea is great, our boats are small.

When homeward bound we gladly turn,
  O bring us safely there,
Where harbor lights of friendship burn
  And peace is in the air.
We trust in Thee, whate'er befall;
Thy sea is great, our boats are small.

Henry Van Dyke

God, God, be lenient her first night there.
The crib she slept in was so near my bed;
Her blue and white wool blanket was so soft;
The pillow hollowed so it fit her head.

Violet Storey

Lord, now lettest thou thy servant depart in peace, according to thy word.

The Bible

Oh, that peace may come!

Queen Victoria, dying

The Lord gave, and the Lord hath taken away; blessed be the name of the Lord.

The Bible

From Lightning and tempest; from plague, pestilence and famine; from battle and murder, and from sudden death, Good Lord, deliver us.

The Book of Common Prayer

O Lord, support us all the day long of this troublous life, until the shades lengthen, and the evening comes, and the busy world is hushed, the fever of life is over, and our work is done. Then, Lord, in thy mercy, grant us safe lodging, a holy rest, and peace at the last; through Jesus Christ our Lord.

Cardinal John Henry Newman

My God, my Father, and my Friend,
Do not forsake me in the end.

Tommaso di Celano

Preparation

The perpetual work of your life is but to lay the foundation of death.

Michel de Montaigne

We could probably prove that throughout history those Christians who have accomplished the most practical benefit in this world are those who have believed most fervently in the next.

Gordon W. Allport

Do not seek death. Death will find you. But seek the road which makes death a fullfilment.

Dag Hammarskjold

When a man knows he is to be hanged in a fortnight, it concentrates his mind wonderfully.

Samuel Johnson

Do you realize the planning that goes into a death? Probably even more than goes into a marriage. This, after all, really is for eternity.

Gail Parent

A wise man's life is all one preparation for death.

Cicero

You have to learn to do every thing, even to die.

Gertrude Stein

If you want to die happily, learn to live; if you would live happily, learn to die.

Celio Calgagnini

It is uncertain where death awaits us; let us await it everywhere. Premeditation of death is premeditation of freedom. He who has learned how to die frees us from all subjection and constraint. There is nothing evil in life for the man who has thoroughly grasped the fact that to be deprived of life is not an evil.

Michel de Montaigne

While I thought that I was learning how to live, I have been learning how to die.

Leonardo da Vinci

One must take all one's life to learn how to live, and what will perhaps make you wonder more, one must take all one's life to learn how to die.

Seneca

"Oh, nobody knows when de Lord is goin ter call,
  Roll dem bones.
It may be in de Winter time, and maybe in de Fall,
  Roll dem bones.
But yer got ter leabe yer baby and yer home and all—
  So roll dem bones."

DuBose Heyward

If thou expect death as a friend, prepare to entertain it;
if thou expect death as an enemy, prepare to overcome it;
death has no advantage, but when it comes as a stranger.

Francis Quarles

Think not disdainfully of death, but look on it with favor, for Nature wills it like all else . . . . Look for the hour when the soul shall emerge from this its sheath, as now thou awaitest the moment when the child she carries shall come forth from thy wife's womb.

Marcus Aurelius

Expect an early death--it will keep you busier.

Martin H. Fisher

Death tugs at my ear and says: "Live, I am coming."

Oliver Wendell Holmes

In sickness the soul begins to dress herself for immortality.

Jeremy Taylor

To think of death and to prepare for death, is not a surrender; it is a victory over fear.

Paul W. von Keppler

Deep within life is the need to orient it toward death. The one incontrovertible item of our knowledge about death is that it gives notice of itself as motion, we go toward it, we go through it. It never loses its goingness.

Mary Austin

The philosopher's whole life is a preparation for death.

Cicero

Sleep; and if life was bitter to thee, pardon;
If sweet, give thanks; thou hast no more life;
And to give thanks is good, and to forgive.

Algernon C. Swinburne

Promised Land

The last day does not bring extinction, but change of place.

Cicero

I've got a home out yonder;
Few days, few days;
I've got a home out yonder;
I am going home.

Anonymous

Why is a man and at the end of his life he leaves for his true home in heaven?

The Chofetz Chain

After the royal throne comes death; after the dunghill comes the Kingdom of Heaven.

Saint John Chrysostom

175

Sometimes I see in heaven the shores without end covered with the shining peoples of joy. A great vessel, all gold, above me, flourishes its banners and pennants, multicolored in the morning breeze.

Arthur Rimbaud

Death is the crown of life:
Were death denied, poor man would live in vain;
Were death denied, to live would not be life;
Were death denied, ev'n fools would to die.

Edward Young

Has this world been so kind to you that you should leave it with regret? There are better things ahead than any we leave behind.

Clive S. Lewis

Life is the desert, life the solitude;
Death joins us to the great majority.

Edward Young

Henceforward, listen as we will,
The voices of that heart are still;
Look where we may, the wide earth o'er
Those lighted faces smile no more. . . .
Yet Love will dream, and Faith will trust
(Since He who knows our need is just)
That somehow, somewhere, meet we must.

John Greenleaf Whittier

He is not dead, this friend; not dead,
But, in the path we mortals tread,
Got some few, trifling steps ahead,
    And nearer to the end;
So that you too once past the bend,
Shall meet again, as face to face this friend
    You fancy dead.

Robert Louis Stevenson

Surely there is something pleasing in the belief that our separation from those whom we love is merely corporal; and it may be a great incitement to virtuous friendship if it can be made probable that the union that has received the divine approbation shall continue to eternity.

Samuel Johnson

Oh! when a Mother meets on high
    The Babe she lost in infancy,
Hath she not then, for pains and fears,
    The day of woe, the watchful night,
For all her sorrow, all her tears,
    An over-payment of delight?

Robert Southey

Only faith in a life after death is a brighter world where dear ones will meet again—only that and the measured tramp of time can give consolation.

Churchill

177

I have friends in Spirit Land,
Not shadows in a shadowy band,
No others but themselves are they.
And still I think of them the same
As when the Master's summons came.

John Greenleaf Whittier

And with the morn those angel faces smile
Which I have loved since, and lost awhile.

John H. Newman

It is but crossing with a bated breath,
A white, set face, a little strip of sea—
To find the loved one waiting on the shore,
More beautiful, more precious than before.

Ella Wheeler

Swing low, sweet chariot—
Comin' for to carry me home;
I looked over Jordan and what did I see?
A Band of angels comin' after me—
Comin' for to carry me home.

Black Spiritual

R

READY TO DIE

REJOICING

RELEASE

REMEMBRANCE

REQUIEMS

REST IN PEACE

RESURRECTION

REWARDS IN HEAVEN

ROUND TRIPS

Ready to Die

I have a strong feeling that I shall be glad when I am dead and done for—scrapped at last to make room for somebody better, cleverer, more perfect than myself.

George Bernard Shaw

Death is not the greatest of ills; it is worse to want to die, and not be able to.

Sophocles

For a man who has done his natural duty, death is as natural and welcome as sleep.

George Santayana

The world is but a vale of tears; the sooner we leave it the better.

Perez Galdos

Death is a friend of ours; and he that is not ready to entertain him is not at home.

Francis Bacon

Most people would die sooner than think; in fact, they do.
Bertrand Russell

Beyond the shining and the shading,
Beyond the hoping and the dreading
  I shall be soon.
Love, rest and home!
  Sweet hope!
Lord! tarry not, but come.

Horatius Bonar

Our fear of death is like our fear that summer will be short, but when we have had our swing of pleasures, our fill of fruit, and our swelter of heat, we say we have had our day.

Ralph Waldo Emerson

Nothing you can lose by dying is half so precious as the readiness to die, which is man's charter of nobility.

George Santayana

It is a great consolation to a poet at the point of death that he has never written a line injurious to good morals.

Nicolas Boileau

I enjoy good health; I am happy in what is around me, yet I assure you I am ripe for leaving all this year, this day, this hour.

Thomas Jefferson

No one can be more willing to send me out of life than I am desirous to go.

Archbishop William Laud

If I could drop dead right now, I'd be the happiest man alive!

Samuel Goldwyn

———

How calm and sweet the victories of life,
How terrorless the triumph of the grave.

Percy Bysshe Shelley

———

Under the wide and starry sky,
Dig the grave and let me die.

Robert L. Stevenson

Rejoicing

We rejoice over a birth and mourn over a death. But we should not. For when a man is born, who knows what he will do or how he will end? But when a man dies, we may rejoice—if left a good name and this world in peace.

Midrash

———

I thank God, and with joy I mention it. I was never afraid of Hell, nor ever grew pale at the description of that place, I have so fixed my contemplations on Heaven, that I have almost forgot the Idea of Hell.

Thomas Browne

"Take my own father! You know what he said in his last moments? On his deathbed, he defied me to name a man who had enjoyed a better life. In spite of the dreadful pain, his face radiated happiness!" said Mother, nodding her head comfortably, "Happiness drives out pain, as fire burns out fire."

Mary Lavin

Come lovely and soothing death,
Undulate round the world, serenely arriving, arriving,
In the day, in the night, to all, to each,
Sooner or later delicate death.

Prais'd be the fathomless universe,
For life and joy, and for objects and knowledge curious,
And for love, sweet love—but praise! praise! praise!
For the sure-enwinding arms of cool-enfolding death.

Walt Whitman

We enjoy some gratification when our good friends die; for though their death leaves us in sorrow, we have the consolatory assurance that they are beyond the ills by which in this life even the best of men are broken down or corrupted.

Saint Augustine of Hippo

An odd thing about New Orleans: The cemeteries here are more cheerful than the hotels and the French Quarter. Tell me why that should be, why 2,000 dead Creoles should be more alive than 2,000 Buick dealers?

Walker Percy

Joy, shipmate, joy!
(Pleas'd to my soul at death I cry,)
Our life is closed, our life begins,
The long, long anchorage we leave,
The ship is clear at last, she leaps!
She swiftly courses from the shore,
Joy, shipmate, joy!

Walt Whitman

When I catch myself resenting not being immortal, I pull myself up short by asking whether I should really like the prospect of having to make out an annual income-tax return for an infinite number of years ahead.

Arnold J. Toynbee

Has any one supposed it lucky to be born?
I hasten to inform him or her, it is just as lucky to die, and I know it.

Walt Whitman

If you're not allowed to laugh in heaven, I don't want to go there.

Martin Luther

We weep when we are born, not when we die!

Thomas B. Aldrich

Glory Hallelujah! I am going to the Lord! I come! Ready! Go!

Charles J. Guiteau

Expect no greater happiness in Eternity, than to rejoice in God.

Benjamin Whichcote

Release

Death is the privilege of human nature,
And life without it were not worth our taking:
Thither the poor, the pris'ner and the mourner
Fly for relief, and lay their burthens down.

Nicholas Rowe

Nothing is dead, but that which wished to die;
Nothing is dead, but wretchedness and pain.

Edward Young

Death is sometimes a punishment, often a gift; to many it has been a favor.

Seneca

And God said, Go down, Death, go down;
Go down to Savannah, Georgia,
Down to Yamacraw.
And find Sister Caroline.
She's borne the burden and the heat of the day,
She's Labored long in my vineyard,
And she's tired—
She's weary—
Go down, Death, and bring her to me.

James W. Johnson

Never any weary traveller complained that he came too soon
to his journey's end.

Thomas B. Fuller

Death is the poor man's doctor.

German proverb

There is no unmixed good in this world except dying.

Henry W. Beecher

Why fear death; the mother of rest, death that puts an end to
sickness and the pains of poverty? It happens but once to
mortals, and no man ever saw it come twice.

Agathias

Death is a release from the impressions of the senses, and from the desires that make us their puppets, and from the vagaries of the mind, and from the hard service of the flesh.

Marcus Aurelius

Death is the liberator of him whom freedom cannot release, the physician of him whom medicine cannot cure, and the comforter of him whom time cannot console.

Charles C. Colton

The stroke of death is as a lover's pinch,
Which hurts and is desired.

Shakespeare

If a man knew the gain of death, the ease of death, he would solicit, he would provoke death to assist him, by any hand, which he might use.

John Donne

Why do you weep? Did you think I should live forever? I thought it was more difficult to die.

Louis XIV, King of France

Living is a misfortune, death a kindness.

Giacomo Leopardi

Whoever has lived long enough to find out what life is knows how deep a debt of gratitude we owe to Adam, the first great benefactor of our race. He brought death into the world.

Mark Twain (Samuel Clemens)

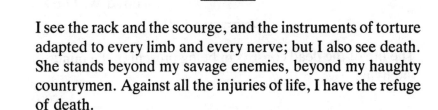

I see the rack and the scourge, and the instruments of torture adapted to every limb and every nerve; but I also see death. She stands beyond my savage enemies, beyond my haughty countrymen. Against all the injuries of life, I have the refuge of death.

Seneca

Death is the only mercy, that I crave,
Death soon and short, death and forgetfulness.

Robert Southey

Remembrance

Him who is dead and gone, honour with remembrance, not with tears.

Saint John Chrysostom

The man who has a grave or two in his heart does not need to haunt churchyards.

Alexander Smith

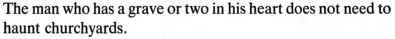

189

We who are left how shall we look again
Happily on the sun or feel the rain
Without remembering how they who went
Ungrudgingly and spent
Their lives for us loved, too, the sun and rain?

Wilfred W. Gibson

The life of the dead consists in being present in the minds of the living.

Cicero

To live in hearts we leave behind,
Is not to die.

Thomas Campbell

To die completely, a person must not only forget but be forgotten, and he who is not forgotten is not dead.

Samuel Butler

The dead abide with us. Though stark and cold,
Earth seems to grip them, they are with us still;
They have forged our chains of being for good or ill,
And their invisible hands these hands yet hold.

Mathilde Blind

It takes time for the absent to assume their true shape in our thoughts. After death they take on a firmer outline and then cease to change.

Sidonie Gabrielle Colette

The record of a generous life runs like a vine around the memory of our dead, and every sweet, unselfish act is now a perfumed flower.

Robert G. Ingersoll

There's one thing that keeps surprising you about stormy old friends after they die—their silence.

Ben Hecht

We miss thy small step on the stair;
We miss thee at thine evening prayer;
All day we miss thee, everywhere.

David M. Moir

How very little the world misses anybody.
How soon the chasm left by the best and wisest men closes.

Thomas B. Macaulay

When good men die their goodness does not perish,
But lives though they are gone.

Euripides

You can lose a man like that by your own death, but not by his.

George Bernard Shaw

Throwing away then all things, hold to these only which are few; and besides bear in mind that every man lives only this present time, which is an indivisible point, and that all the rest of his life is either past or it is uncertain. Short then is the time which every man lives, and small the nook of the earth where he lives; and short too the longest posthumous fame, and even this only continued by a succession of poor human beings, who will very soon die, and who know not even themselves, much less him who died long ago.

Marcus Aurelius

The dead know not anything, neither have they anymore a reward; for the memory of them is forgotten.

The Bible

He shall fly away as a dream, and shall not be found: yea, he shall be chased away as a vision of the night.

The Bible

Requiems

In dreams she grows not older,
  The lands of dream among,
Though all the world wax colder,
  Though all the songs be sung,
In dreams doth he behold her
  Still fair and kind and young.

Andrew Lang

I know thou art gone to the home of thy rest—
  Then why should my soul be so sad?
I know thou art gone where the weary are blest,
  And the mourner looks up, and is glad:
I know thou hast drank of the Lethe that flows
  In the land where they do not forget,
That sheds over memory only repose,
  And takes from it only regret.

Thomas K. Hervey

One more unfortunate,
Weary of breath,
Rashly importunate,
Gone to her death!

Take her up tenderly,
Lift her with care;
Fashion'd so slenderly,
Young, and so fair.

Thomas Hood

Close his eyes; his work is done.
  What to him is friend or foeman,
Rise of moon, or set of sun,
  Hand of man, or kiss of woman?

George H. Boker

King Tety has not indeed died. He has become a glorious one in the sky; he abides in continuity. The lifetime of King Unis is eternity; his boundary is eternity. . . . Though thou sleepest, thou wakest again; though thou diest, thou livest again.

Inscribed on a Royal Egyptian Tomb, c. 2500 B.C.

Weep not, O Friend, we should not weep:
 Our friend of friends lies full of rest;
 No sorrow rankles in her breast,
Fallen fast asleep, She sleeps below
She wakes and laughs above;
To-day, as she walked, let us walk in love;
To-morrow, follow so.

Christina Rossetti

———

Yes, 'twill only be a sleep:
When, with songs and dewy light,
Morning blossoms out of Night,
She will open her blue eyes
'Neath the palms of Paradise,
While we foolish ones shall weep.

Edward R. Sill

———

For some we loved, the loveliest and the best
That from his Vintage rolling time hath prest,
 Have drunk their Cup a Round or two before,
And one by one crept silently to rest.

Omar Khayyam

———

A single death is a tragedy, a million deaths is a statistic.

Joseph Stalin

———

Every death even the cruellest death drowns in the total indifference of Nature. Nature herself would watch unmoved if we destroyed the entire human race.

Peter Weis

It singeth low in every heart,
    We hear it each and all,—
A song of those who answer not,
    However we may call;
They throng the silence of the breast,
    We see them as of yore,—
The kind, the brave, the true, the sweet,
    Who walk with us no more.

                          John W. Chadwick

The silent organ loudest chants
The master's requiem.

                          Ralph Waldo Emerson

Rest In Peace

Blessed are the dead which die in the Lord from henceforth:
Yea, saith the Spirit, that they may rest from their labors;
and their works do follow them.

                                              The Bible

Death is a delightful hiding-place for weary men.

                                              Herodotus

There's no reason to be the richest man in the cemetery. You
can't do any business from there.

                                              Colonel Sanders

Sleep on, beloved, sleep and take thy rest;
Lay down thy head upon thy Saviour's breast;
We love thee well, but Jesus loves thee best—
Good-night! Good-night! Good-night!

> Sarah Doudney

What better can the Lord do for a man, than take him home when he had done his work?

> Charles Kingsley

Out of the strain of the Doing,
Into the peace of the Done;
Out of the thirst of Pursuing,
Into the rapture of Won.

> W.M.L. Jay

Weep not for him who departs from life, for there is no suffering beyond death.

> Palladas

There the wicked cease from troubling: and there the weary be at rest.

> The Bible

The tomb is still the best fortress against the storms of destiny.

> Georg C. Lichtenberg

Be not afraid, ye waiting hearts that weep,
For God still giveth his beloved sleep,
And if an endless sleep He wills, so best.

Henrietta H. Huxley

Bury me where the birds will sing over my grave.

Alexander Wilson

Oh well, no matter what happens, there's always death.

Napoleon Bonaparte

Here she lies a pretty bud,
Lately made of flesh and bloop;
Who, as soon fell fast asleep
As her little eyes did peep.
Give her strewings, but not stir
The earth that lightly covers her.

Robert Herrick

Peace, rest, and sleep are all we know of death,
And all we dream of comfort.

Algernon C. Swinburne

For death there is no medicine.

German proverb

Buddhism . . . is so persuaded of survival after death as being the rule, that it grants only to rare and elect souls the privilege of at length laying down the burden of continuous life.

Ilya I. Metchnikoff

A good life has a peaceful death.

French proverb

His Maker kissed his soul away,
And laid his flesh to rest.

Isaac Watts

Resurrection

After the resurrection of the body shall have taken place, being set free from the condition of time, we shall enjoy eternal life, with love ineffable and steadfastness without corruption.

Saint Augustine of Hippo

The word "death" never occurs in the Pyramid Texts except in the negative or applied to a foe. Over and over again we hear the indomitable assurance that the dead live.

James H. Breasted

We are too stupid about death. We will not learn
How it is wages paid to those who earn,
How it is the gift for which on earth we yearn;
To be set free from bondage for the flesh;
How it is turning seed-corn into grain,
How it is winning Heaven's eternal gain,
How it means freedom evermore from pain.
How it untangles every mortal mesh.

William C. Doane

There is no such thing as death, In nature, nothing dies:
From each sad moment of decay some forms of life arise.

Charles MacKay

If the Father deigns to touch with divine power the cold and
pulseless heart of the buried acorn and to make it burst forth
from its prison walls, will He leave neglected in the earth the
soul of man made in the image of his Creator?

William Jennings Bryan

Death is part of this life and not of the next.

Elizabeth Bibesco

The truest end of Life, is to know the Life that never ends.

William Penn

With Christ's death and resurrection something happened to death. . . . Christ's death has given it a new character, which does not change its form but does alter its meaning and restore it to what it should have been for the first man—the passage into a new, eternally human life.

Romano Guardini

The Bible tells us, and tells us clearly, that by the death of Jesus Christ on the cross, death itself has been conquered, its bitter sting has been removed, and in a day yet to be, it will be destroyed.

Joseph Bayly

Hell is . . . deep, dark, vile—devoid of comfort and happiness—but Hell is not eternal, for there comes at last the day of resurrection and the period of renovation "when the world will be regenerated, and all will be saved by the compassionate Lord."

M. N. Dhalla

I think of death as a glad awakening, from this troubled sleep which we call life; as an emancipation from a world which, beautiful though it be, is still a land of captivity.

Lyman Abbott

If a man will link himself to the will of God and the reign of God over all human affairs; if he lives for it, dies for it, life and death are merged in the life and purpose of God and therefore he is indestructible.

John Gardiner

No one who is fit to live need fear to die. . . . To us here, death is the most terrible word we know. But when we have tasted its reality, it will mean to us birth, deliverance, a new creation of ourselves.

George S. Merriam

I believe with perfect faith that there will be a revival of the dead at the time when it shall please the Creator.

Maimonides

Peace, Peace! He is not dead, he doth not sleep—
He hath awakened from the dream of life.

Percy Bysshe Shelley

Safe from temptation, safe from sin's pollution,
She lives, whom we call dead.

Henry Wadsworth Longfellow

Passed from death unto life.

The Bible

Rewards In Heaven

Wherefore I praised the dead which are already dead, more than the living which are yet alive.

The Bible

Since in the course of our life here below virtue is not duly rewarded, there must be a future life in which a Sovereign Ruler complete His sanction on the moral order by giving to each according to his deserts.

Désiré Joseph Mercier

If you wish to make a man look noble, your best course is to kill him. What superiority he may have inherited from his race, what superiority nature may have personally gifted him with, comes out in death.

Alexander Smith

To whom life is heavy, the earth will be light.

Henryk Sienkiewicz

Death, who sets all free,
Hath paid his ransom now, and full discharge.

John Milton

He who, seeking his own happiness, does not punish or kill beings who long for happiness will find happiness after death.

Dhammapada

It is right to wish for death, inasmuch as it is the consummation of our repentance, the entrance to blessedness, and our eternal reward.

Fénelon

And ye now therefore have sorrow: but I will see you again, and your heart shall rejoice, and your joy no man taketh from you. And in that day ye shall ask me nothing. Verily, verily, I say unto you, Whatsoever ye shall ask the Father in my name, he will give it to you. Hitherto have ye asked nothing in my name: ask, and ye shall receive, that your joy may be full.

The Bible

As a well-spent day brings happy sleep, so life well-used brings happy death.

Leonardo da Vinci

What'er thou lovest, man, that, too, become thou must—God, if thou lovest God; dust, if thou lovest dust.

Johann Scheffler

How beautiful is death, when earn'd by virtue!

Joseph Addison

The pain is brief, but the joy eternal!

Johann C.F. von Schiller

Round Trips

The end of birth is death; the end of death is birth: this is ordained!

Edwin Arnold

Our final experience, like our first, is conjectural. We move between two darknesses.

Edward M. Forster

From the day of your birth you begin to die as well as to live.

Michel de Montaigne

At end of Love, at end of Life,
At end of Hope, at end of Strife,
At end of all we cling to so—
The sun is setting—must we go?

At dawn of Love, at dawn of Life,
at dawn of Peace that follows Strife,
At dawn of all we long for so—
The sun is rising—let us go.

Louise Chandler Moulton

After your death you will be what you were before your birth.

Arthur Schopenhauer

The grave is but a covered bridge leading from light to light, through a brief darkness.

Henry Wadsworth Longfellow

Death borders upon our birth, and our cradle stands in the grave.

Joseph Hall

We have a winding sheet in our Mother's womb, which grows with us from our conception, and we come back into the world, wound up in that winding sheet, for we come to seek a grave.

John Donne

The babe is at peace within the womb,
The corpse is at rest within the tomb;
We begin in what we end.

Percy Bysshe Shelley

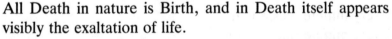

I came from God, and I'm going back to God, and I won't have any gaps of death in the middle of my life.

George Macdonald

I think when men die they do what the trees do in winter when they go dry, but then spring comes and they're reborn. So life must be something else.

Oriana Fallaci

All Death in nature is Birth, and in Death itself appears visibly the exaltation of life.

Johann G. Fichte

As in the generation of leaves, so is that of humanity.
The wind scatters the leaves on the ground, but the live
    timber burgeons with leaves again in the season of spring
    returning.
So one generation of men will grow while another dies.

Homer

Why should you not believe you will exist again after this existence, seeing you exist now after non-existence? . . . . Is it harder for God . . . who made your body when it was not, to make it anew when it has been?

Saint Irenaeus

There was a time when we were not: this gives us no concern— why then should it trouble us that a time will come when we shall cease to be?

William Hazlitt

Death is the peak of a life-wave, and so is birth. Death and birth are one.

Abra Hillel Silver

And when I die, and when I'm gone, there'll be one child born and a world to carry one. . . .

Laura Nyro

Every minute dies a man,
Every minute one is born.

Alfred Lord Tennyson

The beginnings and endings of all human undertakings are untidy.

John Galsworthy

Nature forces us to it. Go out of this world, she says, as you entered it. The same passage that you made from death to life, without feeling or fright, make it again from life to death. Your death is a part of the order of the universe; it is a part of the life of the world.

Michel de Montaigne

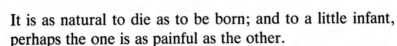

It is as natural to die as to be born; and to a little infant, perhaps the one is as painful as the other.

Francis Bacon

S

SACRIFICE
SALVATION
SHADOWS OF DEATH
SOUL

Sacrifice

Any man's death diminishes me, because I am involved in mankind; and therefore never send to know for whom the bell tolls; it tolls for thee.

John Donne

Our own death is a premium which we must pay for the far greater benefit we have derived from the fact that so many people have not only lived but also died before us.

Samuel Butler

A man who won't die for something is not fit to live.

Martin Luther King, Jr.

There are only war veterans in heaven, who have fought the good fight for the Kingdom of God.

Fulton J. Sheen

The grave of one who dies for truth is holy ground.

German proverb

I die content, I die for the liberty of my country.

Marshal Lannes, dying

Death and wounds will be painful to the brave man and against his will, but he will face them beause it is noble to do so or because it is base not to do so. And the more he is possessed of virtue in its entirety and the happier he is, the more he will be pained at the thought of death; for life is best worth living for such a man, and he is knowingly losing the greatest goods, and this is painful.

Aristotle

Without the hope of immortality, no one would ever face death for his country.

Cicero

We need more courage to die alone. Everybody wants to die with the regiment.

Martin H. Fischer

But we see Jesus, who was made a little lower than the angels for the suffering of death, crowned with glory and honor; that he by the grace of God should taste death for every man.

The Bible

The attitude toward death is changing in our modern thinking. No longer is it something to be feared, but rather a giving of ourselves to God. It is the total gift of ourselves united with Christ.

Clifford Howell

So he died for his faith. That is fine—
  More than most of us do.
But say, can you add to that line
  That he lived for it, too?

Ernest Crosby

She made the stars of heaven more bright
By sleeping under them at night.

George E. Woodberry

Salvation

That which is the end of any natural thing, cannot be evil in itself; since that which is according to nature, is directed to an end by divine providence.

Saint Thomas Aquinas

If God feels toward men as Christ felt, we simply ask ourselves whether such a God could conceivably call men into an existence like human life, and then let them pass out into nothingness.

Francis J. McConnell

It is perfectly clear . . . that the blood of Christ is the sole satisfaction for the sins of believers, the sole expiation, the sole purgation. . . . Purgatory is simply a dreadful blasphemy against Christ.

John Calvin

Let me die the death of the righteous, and let my last end be like his!

The Bible

Our Saviour Jesus Christ . . . hath abolished death, and hath brought life and immortality to light through the gospel.

The Bible

This much, and this is all we know,
They are supremely blest,
Have done with sin, and care, and woe,
And with their Saviour rest.

John Newton

I thank my God heartily that he hath brought me into the light to die, and not suffered me to die in the dark.

Walter Raleigh

Death is the Messiah. That's the real truth.

Isaac Bashevis Singer

Death is no death if it raises us in a moment from darkness to light, from weakness into strength, from sinfulness into holiness. Death is not death, if it brings us nearer to Christ.

Charles Kingsley

And I hear from the outgoing ship in the bay
   The song of the sailors in glee:
So I think of the luminous footprints that bore
   The comfort o'er dark Galilee,
And wait for the signal to go to the shore,
   To the ship that is waiting for me.

Bret Harte

The dead are all holy, even they that were base and wicked while alive. Their baseness and wickedness was not they, was but the heavy and unmanageable environment that lay round them.

Thomas Carlyle

The difficult . . . is not to avoid death, but to avoid unrighteousness; for that runs faster than death.

Plato

To rest in God eternally is the supreme joy of Heaven. Indeed, Heaven has no meaning but that.

Bede Jarrett

He that is dead is freed from sin.

The Bible

Shadows of Death

I have always had a haunting distrust and fear of comfort and warmth because they seem to me a coating, a crust which quickly makes one dull to the reality of real things—like death. It seems to me that the true proportion of realities is that which one must see in the hour of death. If I could only constantly keep that proportion in my mind, I think life would be much greater.

Katharine Butler Hathaway

Live mindful of death.

Persius

It is uncertain where death may await thee, therefore expect it everywhere.

Seneca

On my eyelids is the shadow of death.

The Bible

Death stands above me, whispering low
 I know not what into my ear;
Of his strange language all I know
 Is, there is not a word of fear.

Walter S. Landor

The dead are often just as living to us as the living are, only we cannot get them to believe it. They can come to us, but till we die we cannot go to them. To be dead is to be unable to understand that one is alive.

Samuel Butler

Even in the valley of the shadow of death, two and two do not make six.

Leo Tolstoy

Before I go whence I shall not return, even to the land of darkness and the shadow of death.

The Bible

Like a fish that is thrown on dry land, taken from his home in the waters, the mind strives and struggles to get free from the power of Death.

Dhammapada

Worldly faces never look so worldly as at a funeral.

George Eliot (Mary Ann Evans)

He who lives more lives than one
More deaths than one must die.

Oscar Wilde

. . . Africa seemed the harmonious voice of creation. Everything alive was inextricably intertwined until death. And even
death was part of the life harmony.

Shirley MacLaine

Oh! little did my mother think,
   That day she craddled me,
The lands that I should travel in,
   The deaths that I should see.

Scottish song

Neither in the hearts of men nor in the manners of society will
there be a lasting peace until we outlaw death.

Albert Camus

Death is an angel with two faces:
   To us he turns
A face of terror, blighting all things fair;
   The other burns
With glory of the stars, and love is there.

T.C. Williams

Death is king of the world; 'tis his park
Where he breeds life to feed him. Cries of pain
Are music for his banquet.

George Eliot (Mary Ann Evans)

I'm forty-three years old, and I'm the healthiest candidate for president in the United States. You've traveled with me enough to know that. I'm not going to die in office.

John F. Kennedy

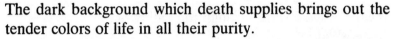

The dark background which death supplies brings out the tender colors of life in all their purity.

George Santayana

Even at our birth, death does but stand aside a little. And every day he looks towards us and muses somewhat to himself whether that day or the next he will draw nigh.

Robert Bolt

The whole of life is a country of vanity, and when we sense the breath of death, we wither away like flowers.

Aleksei Tolstoy

Death is when you get sick one day and you don't get well again. Can't seem to shake it off.

John Phillips

When death lifts the curtain it's time to be startin'.

Scottish proverb

None but those shadowed by death's approach are suffered to know that death is a blessing; the gods conceal this from those who have life before them, in order that they may go on living.

Lucan

Yea, though I walk through the valley of
   the shadow of death,
I will fear no evil: for thou art with me;
thy rod and thy staff they comfort me.

The Bible

Everything mortal can be raised up or laid low in a single day.

Sophocles

Soul

The soul lives forever: it is a portion of the Deity housed in our bodies.

Flavius Josephus

The soul . . . comes directly from God in heaven. . . . The soul is not destroyed, as it does not require physical life for its activities.

Maimonides

When I reflect on the nature of the soul, it seems to me by far more difficult and obscure to determine its character while it is in the body, a strange domicile, than to imagine what it is when it leaves it, and has arrived in the empyreal regions, in its own and proper home.

Cicero

The eternity of the spirit does not begin after death, but is, like God, always present.

Moses Hess

What, I pray you, is dying? Just what it is to put off a garment. For the body is about the soul as a garment; and after laying this aside for a short time by means of death, we shall resume it again with more splendor.

Saint John Chrysostom

How little room
Do we take up in death, that living know
No bounds!

James Shirley

The corpse is not the whole animal.

Johann W. von Goethe

Death, if thou wilt, fain would I plead with thee:
Canst thou not spare, of all our hopes have built,
One shelter where our spirits fain would be,
   Death, if thou wilt?

Algernon C. Swinburne

The soul in its nature loves God and longs to be at one with Him in the noble love of a daughter for a noble father; but coming to human birth and lured by the courtships of this sphere, she takes up with another love, a mortal, leaves her father and falls. But one day coming to hate her shame, she puts away the evil of earth, once more seeks the father, and finds her peace.

Plotinus

If we have but once seen any child of Adam, we have seen an immortal soul. It has not passed away, as a breeze or sunshine, but it lives; it lives at this moment in one of those many places, whether in bliss or misery, in which all souls are reserved until the end.

John H. Newman

The body dies but the spirit is not entombed.

Dhammapada

There is a part of the soul that is untouched by time or mortality: it proceeds out of the Spirit and remains eternally in the Spirit and is divine.

Meister Eckhart

The death . . . of the soul takes place when God forsakes it, as the death of the body when the soul forsakes it.

Saint Augustine of Hippo

The meaning of death is not the annihilation of the spirit, but its separation from the body, and that the resurrection and day of assembly do not mean a return to a new existence after annihilation, but the bestowal of a new form or frame to the spirit.

                                                                    Al-Ghazzali

Death with the might of his sunbeam,
Touches the flesh, and the soul awakes.

                                                                    Robert Browning

Death alone proclaims the insignificance of our poor human bodies.

                                                                    Juvenal

O wretched little soul of mine, imprisoned in an unworthy body, go forth, be free!

                                                                    Cornificia

I swear I think now that everything without exception has
    an eternal soul—
The trees have, rooted in the ground; the weeds of the sea
    have; the animals.

                                                                    Walt Whitman

The root cause of a man's grief and delusion is the identification of the Soul with the body. Fear of death paralyzes him because he is ignorant of the Soul's true nature. The wise perform their duties in the world, cherishing always the knowledge of the Soul's deathlessness.

Swani Nikhilananda

We know that it (the soul) survives the body and that being set free from the bars of the body, it sees with clear gaze those things which before, dwelling in the body, it could not see.

Saint Ambrose

And I say let a man be of good cheer about his soul. When the soul has been arrayed in her own proper jewels—temperance, and justice, and courage, and nobility and truth—she is ready to go on her journey when the hour comes.

Socrates

TOO SOON

Too Soon

It was the eleventh of December,
　On a cold and windy day,
Just at the close of evening,
　When the sunlight fades away;
Little Henry he was dying,
　In his little crib he lay,
With soft winds round him sighing
　From the morn till close of day.

Julia A. Moore

Is life a boon?
If so, it must befall
　That death, whene'er he call,
Must call too soon.

William S. Gilbert

Nothing seems so tragic to one who is old as the death of one
who is young, and this alone proves that life is a good thing.

Zoe Akins

A little soul scarce fledged for earth
　Takes wing with heaven again for goal,
Even while we hailed as fresh from birth
　A little soul.

Algernon C. Swinburne

He seemed a cherub who had lost his way
And wandered hither, so his stay
With us was short, and 'twas most meet,
That he should be no delver in earth's clod,
Nor need to pause and cleanse his feet
To stand before his God.

James R. Lowell

Three years she grew in sun and shower,
Then Nature said, "A lovelier flower
On earth was never sown;
This child I to myself will take;
She shall be mine, and I will make
A Lady of my own."

William Wordsworth

A boy of five years old serene and gay,
Unpitying Hades buried me away.
Yet weep not for Callimachus: if few
The days I lived, few were my sorrows too.

Lucian

Heav'n gave him all at once; then snatch'd away,
Ere mortals all his beauties could survey;
Just like the flower that buds and withers in a day.

John Dryden

I know of nobody that has a mind to die this year.

Thomas B. Fuller

If he died young he lost but little, for he understood but little, and had not capacities of great pleasures or great cares; but yet he died innocent, and before the sweetness of his soul was deflowered and ravished.

Jeremy Taylor

She passed away like morning dew
  Before the sun was high;
So brief her time, she scarcely knew
  The meaning of a sigh.

Hartley Coleridge

Tenderly bury the fair young dead,
  Pausing to drop on his grave a tear;
Carve on the wooden slab at his head,
  "Somebody's darling slumbers here!"

Marie R. La Coste

No sound of tiny footfalls filled the house
With happy cheer.

Robert Buchanan

Old men go to death; death comes to young men.

George Herbert

He whom the gods favor dies young, while he is in his health, has his senses and his judgment sound.

Plautus

Love lent me wings; my path was like a stair;
A lamp unto my feet, that sun was given;
And death was safety and great joy to find;
But dying now, I shall not climb to Heaven.

Michelangelo

Man weeps to think that he will die so soon; woman, that she
was born so long ago.

H.L. Mencken

To die is poignantly bitter, but the idea of having to die
without having lived is unbearable.

Erich Fromm

No one should be allowed to die before he has loved!

Saint John Perse

Life's pleasure hath he lost—escaped life's pain.
Nor wedded joys nor wedded sorrows knew.

Julianus

He that cuts off twenty years of life
Cuts off so many years of fearing death.

Shakespeare

'Whom the gods love die young,' was said of yore,
  And many deaths do they escape by this:
The death of friends, and that which slays even more—
  The death of friendship, love, youth, all that is,
Except mere breath; and since the silent shore
  Awaits at last even those who longest miss
The old archer's shafts, perhaps the early grave
Which men weep over may be meant to save.

Lord Byron

Let us get rid of such old wives' tales as the one that tells us it is tragic to die before one's time. What "time" is that, I would like to know? Nature is the one who has granted us the loan of our lives, without setting any schedule for repayment. What has one to complain of if she calls in the loan when she will?

Cicero

The man who to untimely death is doom'd,
Vainly you hedge him from the assault of harm;
He bears the seed of ruin in himself.

Matthew Arnold

Short is poor man's pleasure here; soon it's gone with no possibility of recall.

Lucretius

It is good to die before one has done anything deserving death.

Anaxandrides

UNCERTAINTIES

Uncertainties

No one knows but that death is the greatest of all good to man; yet men fear it, as if they well knew that it is the greatness of evils. Is not this the more reprehensible ignorance, to think that one knows what one does not know?

Socrates

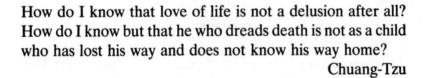

If life were eternal all interest and anticipation would vanish. It is uncertainty which lends its fascination.

Yoshida Kenko

How do I know that love of life is not a delusion after all? How do I know but that he who dreads death is not as a child who has lost his way and does not know his way home?

Chuang-Tzu

If we could know
Which of us, darling, would be first to go,
    Who would be first to breast the swelling tide
    And step alone upon the other side—
If we could know!

Julia Harris May

Our lives are never certain, even for an hour; with tears we come into this world, and with tears we shall leave it.

Ferrant S. Calavera

Man imagines that it is death he fears; but what he fears is the unforeseen, the explosion. What man fears is himself, not death.

Antoine de Saint-Exupéry

Death in itself is nothing; but the fear
To be we know not what, we know not where.

John Dryden

A philosophical contempt of life is no guarantee of courage in the face of death.

Gustave Vapereau

All victory ends in the defeat of death. That's sure. But does defeat end in the victory of death? That's what I wonder!

Eugene O'Neill

There seems to be the same difference between hell, purgatory, and heaven as between despair, uncertainty, and assurance.

Martin Luther

Life and death are balanced on the edge of a razor.

Homer

It has never been satisfactorily determined whether the saying about the darlings of the gods dying young means young in years or young in heart.

Edward V. Lucas

No one can confidently say that he will still be living tomorrow.

Euripides

Without wanting to deceive men, it can be said we have as much reason to believe in as to deny the immortality of the being that thinks.

Voltaire

Now I am about to take my last voyage, a great leap in the dark.

Thomas Hobbes

When I have folded up this tent
  And laid the soiled thing by,
  I shall go forth 'neath different stars,
Under an unknown sky.

Frederick L. Knowles

Dying is a wild night and a new road.

Emily Dickinson

WEEPING AND WAILING
WILLS TO LIVE
WINKING AT DEATH
WISDOM

Weeping and Wailing

Now I have often pondered how it happens that in wars the face of death, whether we see it in ourselves or in others, seems to us incomparably less terrifying than in our houses—otherwise you would have an army of doctors and snivelers—and, since death is always the same, why nevertheless there is much more assurance against it among villagers and humble folk than among others. I truly think it is those dreadful faces and trappings with which we surround it, that frighten us more than death itself; an entirely new way of living; the cries of mothers, wives, and children; the visits of people dazed and benumbed by grief; the presence of a number of pale and weeping servants; a darkened room; lighted candles; our bedside besieged by doctors and preachers; in short, everything horror and fright around us. There we are already shrouded and buried. Children fear even their friends when they see them masked, and so do we ours. We must strip the mask from things as well as from persons; when it is off, we shall find beneath only that same death which a valet or a mere chambermaid passed through not long ago without fear. Happy the death that leaves no leisure for preparing such ceremonies!

Michel de Montaigne

Groans and convulsions, and discolor'd faces,
Friends weeping round us, blacks, and obsequies,
Make death a dreadful thing. The pomp of death
Is far more terrible than death itself.

Nathaniel Lee

They've great respect for the dead in Hollywood, but none for the living.

Errol Flynn

No lamentation can loose
Prisoners of death from the grave.

Matthew Arnold

It is of no avail to weep for the loss of a loved one, which is why we weep.

Solon

Now let the weeping cease; Let no one mourn again.
These things are in the hands of God.

Sophocles

The dead they cannot rise, an' you'd better dry your eyes,
An' you'd best go look for a new love.

Rudyard Kipling

Wills To Live

Man is the only animal that contemplates death, and also the only animal that shows any sign of doubt of its finality.

William E. Hocking

Why do we have to die? As a kid you get nice little white shoes with white laces and a velvet suit with short pants and a nice collar and you go to college, you meet a nice girl and get married, work a few years and then you have to die.

Mel Brooks

If the rich could hire other people to die for them, the poor could make a wonderful living.

Jewish proverb

How shocking must thy summons be, O Death!
To him that is at ease in his possessions;
Who, counting on long years of pleasure here,
Is quite unfurnish'd for that world to come!

Robert Blair

Even the bold will fly when they see Death drawing in close enough to end their life.

Sophocles

To the psychotherapist an old man who cannot bid farewell to life appears as feeble and sickly as a young man who is unable to embrace it.

Carl G. Jung

Our repugnance to death increases in proportion to our consciousness of having lived in vain.

William Hazlitt

We all labour against our own cure, for death is the cure of all diseases.

Thomas Browne

Living had got to be such a habit with him that he couldn't conceive of any other condition.

Flannery O'Connor

A strange sight, sir, an old man unwilling to die.

Ebenezer Elliot, dying

Nothing can be meaner than the anxiety to live on, to live on anyhow and in any shape.

George Santayana

God, I am travelling out to death's sea,
I, who exulted in sunshine and laughter,
Dreamed not of dying—death is such a waste of me!

John Galsworthy

How foolish is he who, facing death, thinks by his cries to lessen its horror.

Euripides

Those who have endeavoured to teach us to die well, have taught few to die willingly.

Samuel Johnson

Whatever crazy sorrow saith,
No life that breathes with human breath
Has ever truly long'd for death.

Alfred Lord Tennyson

As long as one limb moves, men reject the grave.

Hebrew proverb

Each person is born to one possession which outvalues all the others—his last breath.

Mark Twain (Samuel Clemens)

Death is the final Master and Lord, but Death must await my good pleasure. I command Death because I have no fear of Death, but only love.

Havelock Ellis

On the day of his death, a man feels he has lived but a single day.

Zohar

Oh Death, you can wait: keep your distance!

André Marie de Chénier

The world is a fine place and worth the fighting for and I hate very much to leave it.

Ernest Hemingway

No one's so old that he mayn't with decency hope for one
more day.

Seneca

Winking At Death

Happy the man who has trampled underfoot his fears and can
laugh at the approach of all-subduing death.

Virgil

A belief in hell and the knowledge that every ambition is
doomed to frustration at the hands of a skeleton have never
prevented the majority of human beings from behaving as
though death were no more than an unfounded rumour, and
survival a thing beyond the bounds of possibility.

Aldous Huxley

Man has always been under death's dictatorship, always
questioned it, always challenged it.

Candice Bergen

There is no passion in the mind of the man so weak, but it
mates and masters the fear of death. . . . Revenge triumphs
over death; love slights it; honour aspireth to it; grief flieth to
it.

Francis Bacon

The soldier is convinced that a certain interval of time, capable of being indefinitely prolonged, will be allowed him before the bullet finds him, the thief before he is taken, men in general before they have to die.

Marcel Proust

The waters are rising but I am not sinking.

Catherine Booth

It is impossible that anything so natural, so necessary, and so universal as death should ever have been designed by Providence as an evil to mankind.

Jonathan Swift

I want always to love, always to suffer, always to die without death daring to offer me his refuge.

Pierre Corneille

Insurance is death on the installment plan.

Philip Slater

Everybody wants to go to heaven, but nobody wants to die.

Joe Louis

To himself everyone is an immortal; he may know that he is going to die, but he can never know that he is dead.

Samuel Butler The Younger

A syllogism: other men die, but I
Am not another; therefore I'll not die.

Vladimir Nabokov

Wisdom

. . . for the fear of death is indeed the pretence of wisdom,
and not real wisdom, being a pretence of knowing the unknown; and no one knows whether death, which men in their
fear apprehend to be the greatest evil, may not be the greatest
good.

Plato

A free man thinks of nothing less than of death, and his
wisdom is a meditation not of death but of life.

Spinoza

He who knows the joy of Heaven has no grievance against
Heaven and no grudge against men; he is unembarrassed by
things, and unrebuked by the spirits of the departed.

Chuang-Tzu

The wise in heart mourn not for those who live, nor for those
who die.

Bhagavad-Gita

The wise man is never surprised by death: he is always ready to depart.

Jean de la Fontaine

In the last analysis, it is our conception of death which decides our answers to all the questions that life puts to us.

Dag Hammarskjold

Wisdom is on the lips of those about to die.

French proverb

No rational man can die without uneasy apprehensions.

Samuel Johnson